ETHNOGRAPHIC SURVEY OF AFRICA

Volume 44

THE WOLOF OF SENEGAMBIA

THE WOLOF OF SENEGAMBIA
Western Africa
Part XIV

DAVID P. GAMBLE

LONDON AND NEW YORK

First published in 1967 by the International African Institute.

This edition first published in 2017
by Routledge
2 Park Square, Milton Park, Abingdon, Oxon OX14 4RN

and by Routledge
711 Third Avenue, New York, NY 10017

Routledge is an imprint of the Taylor & Francis Group, an informa business

© 1967 International African Institute

All rights reserved. No part of this book may be reprinted or reproduced or utilised in any form or by any electronic, mechanical, or other means, now known or hereafter invented, including photocopying and recording, or in any information storage or retrieval system, without permission in writing from the publishers.

Trademark notice: Product or corporate names may be trademarks or registered trademarks, and are used only for identification and explanation without intent to infringe.

British Library Cataloguing in Publication Data
A catalogue record for this book is available from the British Library

ISBN: 978-1-138-23217-4 (Set)
ISBN: 978-1-315-30463-2 (Set) (ebk)
ISBN: 978-1-138-24080-3 (Volume 44) (hbk)
ISBN: 978-1-315-28233-6 (Volume 44) (ebk)

Publisher's Note
The publisher has gone to great lengths to ensure the quality of this reprint but points out that some imperfections in the original copies may be apparent.

Disclaimer
The publisher has made every effort to trace copyright holders and would welcome correspondence from those they have been unable to trace.

Publisher's note

Due to modern production methods, it has not been possible to reproduce all the charts which appeared in the original book. Please go to www.routledge.com/Ethnographic-Survey-of-Africa/Forde/p/book/9781138232174 to view them.

ETHNOGRAPHIC SURVEY OF AFRICA

EDITED BY DARYLL FORDE

WESTERN AFRICA
PART XIV

THE WOLOF OF SENEGAMBIA
Together with Notes on the Lebu and the Serer

BY

DAVID P. GAMBLE

LONDON
INTERNATIONAL AFRICAN INSTITUTE
1967

This study is one section of the Ethnographic Survey of Africa which the International African Institute is preparing with the aid of a grant made by the Secretary of State under the Colonial Development and Welfare Acts, on the recommendation of the Colonial Social Science Research Council.

PRINTED IN ENGLAND BY
HAZELL, WATSON & VINEY, LTD
LONDON AND AYLESBURY

FOREWORD

THE International African Institute has, since 1945, been engaged on the preparation and publication of an Ethnographic Survey of Africa, the purpose of which is to present in a brief and readily comprehensible form a summary of available information concerning the different peoples of Africa with respect to location, natural environment, economy and crafts, social structure, political organization, religious beliefs and cults. While available published material has provided the basis for the Survey, a mass of unpublished documents, reports and records in government files and in the archives of missionary societies, as well as field notes and special communications by anthropologists and others, have been generously made available and these have been supplemented by personal correspondence and consultation. The Survey is being published in a number of separate volumes, each of which is concerned with one people or a group of related peoples, and contains a comprehensive bibliography and specially drawn map.

A committee of the Institute was set up under the Chairmanship of the late Professor Radcliffe-Brown, and the Director of the Institute has undertaken the organization and editing of the Survey. The generous collaboration of a number of research institutions and administrative officers in Europe and the African territories was secured, as well as the services of senior anthropologists who have been good enough to supervise and amplify the drafts.

The work of the Survey was initiated with the aid of a grant from the British Colonial Development and Welfare Funds, on the recommendation of the Social Science Research Council, to be applied mainly though not exclusively to work relating to British territories. A further grant from the Sudan Government has assisted in the preparation and publication of sections dealing with that territory.

The Ministère de la France d'Outre-Mer and the Institut Français d'Afrique Noire were good enough to express their interest in the project and through their good offices grants have been received from the Governments of French West Africa and the French Cameroons for the preparation and publication of sections relating to those areas. These sections have been prepared by French ethnologists with the support and advice of the late Professor M. Griaule of the Sorbonne, Mme. Calame-Griaule and Professor Th. Monod, Director of I.F.A.N.

The collaboration of the Belgian authorities in this project was first secured by the good offices of the late Professor de Jonghe, who enlisted the interest of the Commission d'Ethnologie of the Institut Royal Colonial Belge. The collaboration of the Institut pour la Recherche Scientifique en Afrique Centrale has also been readily accorded. Work relating to Belgian territories is being carried out under the direction of Professor Olbrechts at the Centre de Documentation of the Musée du Congo Belge, Tervuren, where Mlle. Boone and members of her staff are engaged on the assembly and classification of the vast mass of material relating to African peoples in the Belgian Congo and Ruanda-Urundi. They work in close collaboration with ethnologists in the field to whom draft manuscripts are submitted for checking.

The International African Institute desires to express its grateful thanks to those official bodies whose generous financial assistance has made the carrying out of this project possible and to the many scholars, directors of research organizations, administrative officers, missionaries, and others who have collaborated in the work and, by granting facilities to our research workers and by correcting and supervising their manuscripts, have contributed so largely to whatever merit the various sections may possess.

Since the unequal value and unsystematic nature of existing material was one of the reasons for undertaking the Survey, it is obvious that these studies cannot claim to be complete or definitive; it is hoped, however, that they will present a clear

v

FOREWORD

account of our existing knowledge and indicate where information is lacking and further research is needed.

In connection with the preparation of this volume we are grateful to the Government of French West Africa for providing a financial contribution towards the publication of sections dealing with territories within that area.

This Survey of the Wolof is based both on the literature and on field work carried out by the author among the Wolof of the Gambia, as the holder of a Colonial Research Fellowship and later with assistance from Colonial Development and Welfare Funds and the Gambia Government, to whom our thanks are due. The author is particularly indebted to Dr. David Ames, whose field notes of work among the Wolof of British and French Salum he has had the benefit of studying. He is also grateful to the Institut Français d'Afrique Noire and its staff for providing facilities during a visit to Senegal, and to Professor Th. Monod, M. A. Hauser, M. Massé, M. P. Mercier, and M. and Mme. S. Sauvageot of I.F.A.N., and to M. Pelissier of the Institut des Hautes Études, Dakar, for their help, and to all who read the manuscript at various stages, made corrections and supplied additional material. For access to Wolof material the author would also like to thank the librarians and staff of the International African Institute, the Institut Français d'Afrique Noire at Dakar, the Royal Anthropological Institute, the Royal Empire Society, the School of Oriental and African Studies, the Society of Friends, and the Keeper of the Archives of the Methodist Missionary Society in London.

A list of sections already published in the Ethnographic Survey series will be found on pp. 108–10.

DARYLL FORDE,
Director,
International African Institute.

INTRODUCTION

It is not a simple matter to generalize about the Wolof. Their culture now spans an enormous range, from small rural villages where old ways predominate to modern cities like Dakar; from illiteracy to college training; from lineage and village headship to political parties and ministerial government; from traditional entertainments to radios and football. Even within rural Wolof society there is considerable variation, the values of those of aristocratic origin differing from those descended from former slaves. Neighbouring peoples, Mauretanians to the north, Torobe (Tukulor) to the north-east, Serer to the south-west, Mandinka to the south, have all had some influence on the culture of neighbouring Wolof areas. Variations in environmental conditions—soil, and more especially rainfall and availability of water, as well as proximity to means of transportation (rivers, railways, ports) are reflected in their types of settlement, population movements, and their economic life.

In some parts of the Senegal much of the old Wolof culture is disappearing before both French education on the one hand and the influence of Islam on the other, while elsewhere it has such a high prestige value that other peoples as they progress from more primitive cultures adopt much of the Wolof way of life, so that one finds Serer who now speak only Wolof, Futa Jalon Fulbe who have copied Wolof house styles and furnishings, traders of Jola origin who are not easily distinguishable from Wolof, and so on.

The variability in Wolof culture means that almost every statement made about them needs to be accompanied by a label as to time and place.

As modern published information on the Wolof of Senegal is very scanty, most of the more detailed descriptions given, unless otherwise specified, refer to the Wolof of the Salum area.

NOTE ON ORTHOGRAPHY

The orthography of Wolof has presented a number of problems; something of the confusion which exists can be seen in the table on p. 22. In this study the following sounds have been distinguished:

ε represents an " open " *e* as in *get*
ɔ represents an " open " *o* as in *got*
ŋ represents *ng* as in *sing*
h represents the sound of *ch* as in *loch* (*x* in phonetic script)
ch represents the sound of *ch* as in *church* (*c* in phonetic script)
j tends towards a *dy* sound

It should be noted that *ny* (pronounced like the *ni* in *onion*) is frequently used terminally in Wolof. This does *not* represent the *ny* found terminally in English.

In the literature, however, a number of words occur which were not found in the field. When such words have been used the original spelling of the author concerned has been retained, but the word put in quotation marks. As regards place names, the forms appearing on the maps have usually been followed whether phonetically correct or not. Generally the French spellings have been kept, and only a few of the commonest names and those found in the Gambia have been anglicized. In spelling the names of historical and legendary characters, an attempt has been made to reduce most of them to the script adopted in this report, but complete accuracy cannot be guaranteed.

The spelling of Lebu and Serer names and titles generally follows that of the original sources.

vii

CONTENTS

	PAGE
FOREWORD	v
INTRODUCTION	vii
NOTE ON ORTHOGRAPHY	vii
GROUPING AND DEMOGRAPHY	11

Nomenclature
Distribution
Maps of the area
Demography : population ; density ; migrations ; size of settlements
Tribal intermixture
Physical characteristics

HISTORY AND TRADITIONS OF ORIGIN	16

Origins
The traditional origin of Wolof rule
History : general outlines ; history of the southern zone (Sine-Salum)

LANGUAGE	22

Literature : proverbs ; riddles ; secret languages ; stories ; legends,
history, etc. ; songs ; religious literature ; school books

PHYSICAL ENVIRONMENT	28

Climate : seasons ; rainfall
Vegetation

ECONOMY	29

Crops
Farming methods
Agriculture in the northern zone
Farming calendar
Livestock
Organization and division of labour
Land tenure
Trade
Fishing
Hunting
Natural products
Food and drink : kola nuts ; tobacco
Crafts : blacksmiths ; silversmiths and goldsmiths ; pottery ; leather-
work ; weaving ; dyeing ; basketwork ; woodwork ; hairdressing
Settlements and housing : rural settlements ; urban houses

CONTENTS—*continued*

	PAGE
SOCIAL ORGANIZATION AND POLITICAL SYSTEM	44

Social organization
Social stratification
Descent groups
Terms of kinship and affinity
Local groups : the village ; village groups
Mobility
Age grouping
Marriage
Joking relationships
Friendship
Political system : chieftainship, and government in the Wolof states
Law : civil disputes ; criminal procedure ; marriage law
Inheritance

	PAGE
LIFE CYCLE	62

Birth
Naming ceremony
Wolof names
Carrying a child for the first time
Circumcision
Marriage : betrothal ; *taka* (tying the marriage) ; the marriage-payments ; **mur** (covering the bride) or *chet* ; other forms of marriage
Death

	PAGE
RELIGION	70

Islam
Pagan beliefs and practices
Christianity

	PAGE
OTHER CULTURAL FEATURES	73

Dress and appearance
Character
Etiquette
Hygiene
Entertainments : dancing ; drumming ; singing ; other musical instruments ; wrestling ; play-acting ; miscellaneous games ; horsemanship ; lanterns

	PAGE
CHANGING SOCIAL CONDITIONS	79

	PAGE
BIBLIOGRAPHIES	81

Linguistic material : vocabularies, dictionaries, grammars, etc.
Religious literature
General bibliography

CONTENTS—*continued*

PAGE

A NOTE ON THE LEBU **93**

Distribution and population figures
Language
Origins
History
Physical type
Character
Economic life
Social and political organization
Religion
Changes in Lebu society

Bibliography

A NOTE ON THE SERER 97

Introduction
Nomenclature
Distribution
Demography : population ; density ; vital statistics
Houses and settlements
Physical characteristics
Grouping
Tribal intermixture
Traditions of origin, early movements and inter-tribal relationships
Language
Economy
Political organization
Social organization
Religious beliefs and cults
Dress and appearance

Linguistic bibliography
General bibliography

INDEX 106–7

MAP . . . . at end

GROUPING AND DEMOGRAPHY

NOMENCLATURE

The Wolof refer to themselves as either *Wɔlɔf* or *Ɔlɔf*. Educated Africans in Bathurst, when speaking English, often use the term *Jɔlɔf*, though this is properly the name of the chiefdom (Djolof) from which Wolof domination spread.

A large number of variants on the name occur in the literature. The name *Jalof* first appears in the writings of Cada Mosto (1455); Fernandes (1510) writes of the Kingdom of Gyloffa and refers to the people as *Gyloffes*. Marmol (16th century) uses *Gelofes*, sometimes *Chelofes* or *Ialofes*. De la Courbe (1685) writes *Galofes;* Adanson (1759) calls the natives of Oualo " Oualofes . . . or by corruption *Jallofs.*" Moore, who was in the Gambia in 1730, refers to the Wolof as *Jolloiffs*. Saugnier (1791) *Yolof;* Park (1799) *Jaloffs* or *Yaloffs;* Golberry (1802) *Iolof;* Durand (1806) *Yolof;* Mollien (1820) *Joloffs;* Dard (1826) *Wolof;* Roger (1828) *Ghiolofs*—the *ghi* having the sound as in Italian; Morgan (1864) *Jaloofs;* and in various Gambian Annual Reports, *Yuloff, Joluf, Wollufs,* etc.

Kobès in his dictionary gives both *Olof* and *Volof,* the *v* in his orthography being equivalent to an English *w.* Modern French writers normally use the form *Wolof,* though a few write *Ouolof.* Cheikh Anta Diop is the only author to write *Valaf.*

To the Mandinka Wolof are known as *suruwalu* (sing. *suruwa*); to the Fulbe as *jɔlfube* (sing. *jɔlfo*).

DISTRIBUTION

The region occupied by the Wolof consists of Walo,[1] Kayor,[2] Jolof,[3] part of Baol,[4] and Sine[5]-Salum.[6] It is limited on the north by the River Senegal, which separates the Wolof from the Mauretanians; on the west by the Atlantic; on the south by the Gambia. This area is roughly 220 kilometres from north to south and 150 from east to west.[7] Originally the Wolof occupied an area on the north bank of the Senegal, but were driven south by the Mauretanians. For the Senegal a detailed list of the cantons in which Wolof are found is given by de Tressan.[8]

In the Gambia the Wolof are to be found chiefly in Upper and Lower Salum, the Sabah and Sanjal areas of Upper Badibu, the northern parts of Niani and of Sami, and in Nyomi and Jokadu. In recent years many Wolof have moved from Salum to Niamina East on the south bank of the river. Bathurst is also predominantly a Wolof town, but the people are of different origins from the Salum Wolof, the ancestors of many having come from Gorée, when Bathurst was founded in 1816.

MAPS OF THE AREA

(a) Maps appearing in books and periodicals (for details see bibliography):
" Isles du Cap Verd, Coste, and Pays des Nègres aux environs du Cap Verd." By Sanson d'Abbeville (1656) in Marmol.
Adanson (1759)—map dated 1756 (by Buache) of Senegambia.
Mollien (1820)—map of Senegambia.
Bourgeau (1933)—map of Senegambia dated 1865.
Rousseau (1929)—map of Walo (p. 211).
(1931)—map of Toube (p. 364).
(1933)—map of Kayor (p. 240).

---

[1] Walo = Oualo = Hoval (Labat II 152) = Oval (Labat II 184).
[2] Kayor = Cavord (Pruneau de Pommegorge). Some speakers call it Kajor.
[3] Jolof = Djolof = Guiolof (Labat).
[4] Baol = Bahol (Pruneau de Pommegorge).
[5] Sine is the modern French spelling. Phonetically it should be Siin.
[6] Salum = Saloum.
[7] Bérenger-Féraud, 1879, p. 2.
[8] 1953, pp. 146–50.

THE WOLOF OF SENEGAMBIA

Robin (1946)—sketch map of Walo (p. 256).
Sarr (1949)—sketch of Sine-Salum (p. 833).

(b) General maps:
IFAN. Carte des groupes ethniques d'Afrique Occidentale. (Feuille No. 1)
—1952.
IFAN. Carte demographique d'Afrique Occidentale. (Feuille No. 1)
—1952.

DEMOGRAPHY

Population

Source	Year	Estimated Number
Lasnet	1900	440,000
Le Gouvernement général de l'A.O.F.	1926	450,000
L'encyclopédie coloniale et maritime	1949	660,000
Ethnologie de l'Union Française..	1953	670,000
Guid'A.O.F.	1956–57	709,000

The figure of 843,559 (1950), given by de Tressan, seems to relate to Wolof speakers, and includes 61,124 Lebu.

In the Gambia the Wolof form about one-seventh of the population, the latest figures being:—

Source	Year	Estimated Number
Protectorate (Assessment)	1954	35,670
Bathurst (Census)	1951	9,544
Kombo St. Mary (Census)	1951	1,237
		46,451

Density

A population density map, which includes the Wolof area, has been published (IFAN Carte demographique. Feuille No. 1), but no statistics appear to be available for the Wolof as such. Brasseur (1952, p. 67), writing of the Senegal, states that very roughly the region between the 300° and 600 mm. isohyets (mean annual rainfall) corresponds to a density of about 20 persons per square kilometre,[10] while to the south, where the rainfall is from 600 to 900 mm., it is double—40 to the square kilometre. In the Gambia where the rainfall is about 1,050 mm., the average for the predominantly Wolof region (Sabach, Sanjal, Lower Salum, Upper Salum) is about 45 to the square kilometre, though this is by no means evenly spread and varies from 25 in Sabah to 100 in the Kau-ur—Simbara Valley.

The density is also affected by the means of communication. Along the railway line from Tivaouane to Louga it is between 20 and 35 per square kilometre, while 20 kilometres or so away from the line it drops to between 10 and 20. North of the Thiès–Kaolack line it is between 35 and 50, decreasing to between 20 and 35 farther away, while south of the line it is over 50.

Migrations

According to Sabatié (1926, p. 297) the Wolof once occupied the greater part of Fouta (i.e., Futa Toro) and a vast territory on the north bank of the lower Senegal. Kayor was at that time occupied by Serer and Mandinka. The Fulbe invasion of Futa Toro drove the Wolof westwards, while the Berber and Arab invasions drove those in Ganar (Mauretania) towards the south.[11] These in turn drove the Serer and Mandinka (Sose) towards the Gambia and took possession of

[9] 300 mm. = 12 inches
[10] 20 persons per square kilometre = 50 per square mile.
[11] Presumably in the 14th and 15th centuries.

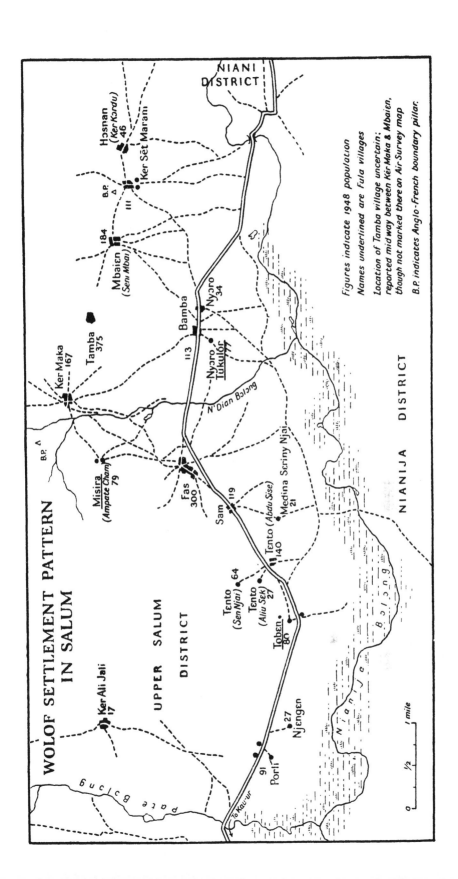

THE WOLOF OF SENEGAMBIA

the territory they occupy to-day. The establishment of the French on the coast and the development of trade led to the growth of the states of Kayor and Baol, and the relative isolation of Jolof.

Before the establishment of the French Protectorate, Wolof attempts to move south into Serer country met with intense resistance and expansion tended to go eastwards, but after the pacification of Serer country, a gradual infiltration began to take place, and with the development of transport services in the Kaolack region a considerable migration has taken place from the regions of Saint-Louis, Louga, and Tivaouane to the southern zone, where the rainfall is heavier and more reliable, and the soils are richer.

At the present time, under the influence of the Mourides (see p. 70), there is a movement of Wolof colonization towards the east, opening up new lands hitherto deserted.

Size of Settlements

In both the Senegal and Gambia Wolof villages are generally small, the average size being less than 100 people. In 1947 Gambian Upper Salum Assessment figures showed only five villages out of 59 with more than 200 people, only one exceeding 300. For the Senegal Rousseau gives the average of 64 villages in 1933 as 95, and of a second sample of 81 villages as 111. As Wolof villages grow larger they tend to break up and form several distinct settlements. The settlement pattern in part of Gambian Salum is shown on the map on page 13.

TRIBAL INTERMIXTURE

Fernandes (1506-10, p. 7), writing of the Kingdom of " Gyloffa," says, " (it) extends from the river (i.e., Senegal) and reaches to the River Gambia, which is also called Cantor, although there are there other peoples like the Barbacijs and the Tucurooes, etc. However all are Gyloffes." The Barbacijs are presumably the inhabitants of Sine, i.e., the Serer, and the Tucurooes, the Tukulor or Futa Toro Fulbe. This would imply that Wolof domination had spread over the Serer area even at this date. Marmol, writing at the end of the 16th century (Vol.III, p. 74), repeats this view " on les nomme toutes ensembles Gélofes dont les principales du costé de Sénéga, sont les Barbacins, les Tucorons, les Saragoles, & les Baganes. . . . Toute la contrée donc, qui est entre ces deux rivières . . . est nommée Gélofes, & ses peuples de même. . . ."

The legends and traditions of the Wolof[12] contain numerous references to migrations and conquests in which many elements—Serer, Fulbe, Mauretanian, Mandinka (Sose) were involved. There are traditions of non-Wolof peoples being absorbed into Wolof communities. The *gelowar*, who became the rulers of Sine-Salum, were reputed to be of Mandinka origin, but are now often considered as Wolof. During the latter part of the 19th century many Jola were captured in wars and raids south of the Gambia, sold as slaves to the Wolof and absorbed into their communities.

Joire (1951, p. 273) thinks that the present-day Wolof are Serer more or less mixed with foreign elements, Mauretanian, Fulbe, Mandinka, Serahuli, and Bambara. This is an extreme view, but in the Wolof culture area there are features almost certainly derived from these peoples—Islam and law from the Mauretanians, groundnut and rice farming techniques from Serahuli and Mandinka, and so on. In fact Wolof culture has very little that is not shared in some degree by neighbouring peoples. Islam has brought the same set of beliefs, similar dress, etiquette, etc., to Mandinka, Fulbe, Serahuli, and Wolof alike. Many Wolof techniques, smithing, leatherwork, etc., have nothing that is specific about them. The pattern of export and import trade, and the modern system of government are common to the Wolof and other Senegambian peoples. In their ceremonies,

[12] See especially Rousseau, 1941-2, pp. 124–35.

GROUPING AND DEMOGRAPHY

naming, marriage, circumcision, etc., there are extremely close parallels to Mandinka and Fulbe custom. Their language, however, distinguishes them from surrounding peoples.

PHYSICAL CHARACTERISTICS

Owing to the long history of local wars and conquests, slave trading in former days, and the gradual absorption of immigrants, one would hesitate to maintain that the Wolof are a homogeneous group. Yet they still stand out in contrast to their neighbours to the north—the Mauretanians, as well as to the light-skinned Fulbe, and to the short, thick-set peoples such as the Jolas and Manjagos south of the Gambia.

In general the men are tall and well built, with broad shoulders, narrow waists, and long thin limbs. Lips are generally less everted than those of the Negro of the rain forest zone, and the nose is often fine, the profile being in many cases slightly aquiline, but whereas the Mauretanians and Fulbe are light in colour, the skin colour of the Wolof is very black.

There are practically no scientific data available on the physical anthropology of the Wolof. A few figures based on small and rather dubious samples are quoted by Hovelacque (1889, p. 3); while fairly detailed anatomical descriptions are given by Bérenger-Féraud (1879, pp. 2-4) and Lasnet (1900, pp. 112-15). The only modern data available are the figures given by Pales (1952). The men in his sample have an average height of 171.58 cm. and a cephalic index of 76.7.

HISTORY AND TRADITIONS OF ORIGIN

Origins

Nothing is really known of the origins of the Wolof. The earliest known inhabitants of the area left traces on beach sites where pottery and polished stone axes are to be found. Shell heaps, stone circles, and tumuli are relatively modern. Joire (1955) considers that the tumuli excavated near Rao might have been constructed in the 14th century, prior to the emergence of the Wolof as a recognizable entity.

Parker (1923) in his account of stone circles in the Gambia mentions that rites were performed at some of the circles to ensure the benevolence of spirits believed to dwell there, but among the present-day Wolof little interest is shown in them, and they have no traditions associating the circles with their own ancestors, generally attributing their construction to the Jola who now dwell on the south bank of the Gambia.

The earliest mention of the name Wolof appears in the writings of Cada Mosto (1455-57), who provided a description of the political organization[1] which corresponds closely with that recorded at a later date. Cada Mosto mentions that the coastal area was inhabited by two nations—one called Barbasini;[2] the other Serreri, which had not been conquered by the Wolof.

Joire (1951) regards the establishment of the Wolof Empire as relatively late, and associated with upheavals and movements of population in the Senegal region as a result of the fall of the Empire of Ghana under the blows of the Almoravides, and then of the Sudanic conquerors, Sumanguru Kante, and Sunjata Keta, about 1240.

Traditions quoted by Robin (1946) for Walo mention that the first inhabitants were Sose (Mandinka), Serer, and Peul (Fulbe), who came from the north. The Wolof appeared, displacing the Sose and many of the Serer, who, however, remained independent in areas difficult of access. At a later date the Wolof in their turn were subject to pressure from the Mauretanians to the north.

The Traditional Origin of Wolof Rule[3]

Tradition has it that the villages of the Jolof area were once independent, each being governed by a chief with the title of *laman* (a Serer term), who acted in consultation with the elders. One day a quarrel arose between neighbouring villages in Walo over wood which was being gathered on the banks of a lake. Bloodshed was threatened when suddenly a man arose from the waters, divided the wood among the parties, and returned to the lake without uttering a word. The people were filled with awe and astonishment at this apparition. Wishing to see if this mysterious person would reappear, they feigned a quarrel and when he again emerged from the water to mediate, they forcibly detained him. They wished to make him their chief, but he was reluctant to stay and remained for several days without eating. So all the women and girls of the neighbourhood were brought to see if any of them could induce him to eat and to stay. He was seen to be moved by the sight of one beautiful girl, she was given to him in marriage and he consented to stay, gradually becoming more human. Details of this apparition were reported to the ruler of Sine, at that time the greatest magician in the land. On learning of the events that had taken place he exclaimed " Ndyadyane Ndyaye", apparently an expression of great astonishment, and the mysterious being was sub-

---

[1] See pp. 55–6.
[2] Barbasini, see p. 17.
[3] The earliest account of this story that I have seen is that given by R. G. V., 1814. It is repeated by Shoberl, Boilat, 1853, and Bérenger-Féraud, 1879.

HISTORY AND TRADITIONS OF ORIGIN

sequently known by this name. The ruler of Sine suggested that Ndyadyane Ndyaye[4] should be appointed head of all the Wolof, and sent tribute as a sign of his submission, the chiefs of other areas following his example.

HISTORY

The history of the Wolof States is a succession of conquests, revolutions, invasions, rebellions, and usurpations. Its elucidation is still further complicated by the orthography of the early writers whose spellings of the names of the characters involved varies from author to author, as well as by confusion between personal names, titles, and place names.

Apart from the writings of early travellers, the main sources are: Faidherbe, who prepared a history of the chiefs of Kayor (1883); Yoro Dyao, a Wolof chief who lived from about 1847 to 1919, who set out to prepare a history of the Wolof, and whose notes were subsequently published and analysed by Gaden[5] and Rousseau.[6] These works should be consulted by those requiring further details. The history of French expansion in the Senegal is described by Sabatié.

General Outlines

The broad outlines are that Wolof domination spread from Jolof until five major states[7]—Kayor, Baol, Walo, Sine and Salum, together with Jolof itself, owed allegiance to its ruler who had the title of *Burba Jɔlɔf*.[8]

One of the earliest accounts of Wolof rulers is to be found in the writings of Marmol (16th century), who describes how a ruler Borbiram (= Bur Biram) was succeeded by his son Biram in 1481. After he had become *bur*, Biram favoured his brother by the same mother, Bemoy (i.e., *bumi,* heir), to the detriment of his brothers by the same father, but different mother, who revolted and deposed him, Bemoy fleeing to Portugal to ask for assistance.

In the 16th century (*c.* 1566) the people of Kayor revolted and became independent, their leader taking the title of *Damɛl* of Kayor.[9] Subsequently he conquered Baol,[10] also becoming *Teny*[11] of Baol, and defeated an army from Jolof which had invaded Kayor, killing the *Burba Jɔlɔf*. The other Wolof rulers refused to acknowledge the *Damɛl* as their head and formed independent states. Their rulers were known as the *Brak* of Walo, the *Bur Sin,*[12] and *Bur Salum*[13] (or *Bar Sin* and *Bar Salum* in Serer). In the north-east the Fulbe invaded Bondu and the banks of the Senegal. Even after the dismemberment of the Wolof empire, the rulers of the various states acknowledged the *Burba Jɔlɔf* as head of the Wolof and continued to pay signs of deference and respect.

By the 17th century when trade with Europeans had developed, Jolof had been cut off in the interior, with no trading port either on the coast or the banks of the Senegal[14] and its prosperity and strength began to decline, while the power and wealth of Kayor and Baol increased.

---

[4] Rousseau, 1929, p. 136.

[5] Gaden: "Légendes et coutumes sénégalaises." *Rev. d'Eth. et de Sociol.,* 1912.

[6] See bibliography.

[7] See diagrams on p. 18 for the broad outlines of these states in former times.

[8] It is difficult to know whether the *ba* in *burba* is merely the Wolof determinative particle for an object at a distance, the Mandinka word for big (Dapper, 1686, speaks of "le Grand Jalof "), or an essential part of the title.

[9] Cada Mosto's Budomel is presumably the *Damɛl*. This would indicate that the title was in existence before the revolt of Kayor. In the English translation of Le Maire he even appears as the "King of Amel."

[10] Diop, 1949, p. 851.

[11] Tègne (Boilat); Teigne (Lasnet, Yoro Dyao); Tin (Golberry); Theim of Baule (De la Courbe); Tènye (Gaden); Taïn (Dapper); Train (Barbot).

[12] Barbasini (Cada Mosto); Bourchin and Barbechin (De la Courbe); Bre (Yoro Dyao); Barbessin (Labat); Bour Sine.

[13] Bursall (Jobson); Bresalme (De la Courbe); Barsally (Moore); Brussalum (Labat); Bre (Yoro Dyao); Bursally (William Smith).

[14] De la Courbe. 1685, pp. 69–70.

B

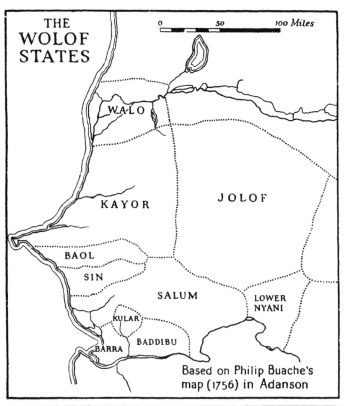
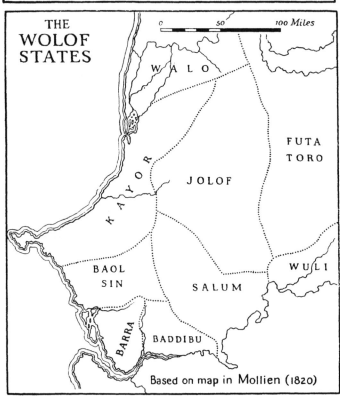

HISTORY AND TRADITIONS OF ORIGIN

The Wolof had become increasingly subject to attacks from the Mauretanians. De la Courbe (1685)[15] mentions that in the 1670s Mauretanian marabouts had instigated a revolt of the people against the kings, promising that if they rebelled the marabouts would make the millet grow without planting by their prayers and magical powers. The rulers of Walo and Kayor were killed and the *Burba Jolof* defeated in battle. The millet failed to grow, and after suffering considerable hardship and famine, the people turned against the Mauretanians and re-elected kings from the royal families. These gathered troops, reconquered their realms, and drove the Mauretanians north of the Senegal.

In 1686 Baol revolted against Kayor.[16] The rulers of Jolof made various attempts to regain control over their former vassal states. Towards the end of the 17th century the *Burba Jolof* attacked Kayor[17] and killed the *Damɛl*. Many of the people fled to Baol and sought the protection of the *Teny*, who took up arms against Jolof, killing the *Burba* in battle. The *Teny* (Latir Fal Sukabe), aided by his army, proceeded to seize power in Kayor, taking the title of *Damɛl*, and appointing two lieutenant-generals (*jambur*) in charge of Kayor and Baol. He maintained power by arranging the death of all nobles considered powerful enough to revolt against him or who offended him in any way, though some escaped by fleeing to neighbouring states, and obtained popular support by forbidding the nobles to exact traditional dues from their vassals. The people were no better off as the *Damɛl* merely took for himself what had formerly belonged to the nobles. After the death of Latir Fal Sukabe in 1702, his sons succeeded him, the eldest becoming *Damɛl* of Kayor, the second *Teny* of Baol.

In the middle of the 18th century Walo was again continually attacked by Mauretanians.[18] In 1786 the *Damɛl* seized Baol,[19] and shortly afterwards was engaged in a war with Almani Abdulkader, ruler of Futa Toro, whom he defeated.[20] In 1790 the people of the Cap Vert peninsula began their struggle for independence from Kayor.[21]

The 19th century saw the gradual expansion of French rule. Cap Vert peninsula finally freed itself from Kayor in 1810 and formed a federation under the presidency of the chief of Dakar, elected from the family of Diop. The French gradually moved from the isle of Gorée to the mainland, taking effective possession of the peninsula in 1857, and creating the port of Dakar in 1859. Walo was annexed in 1866, Kayor in 1883.

After the annexation of Kayor, Jolof remained independent, though the ruler Ali Bouri Njai had been appointed in 1875 under French auspices. But from 1885 his kingdom became the refuge of elements hostile to France, and he formed alliances with turbulent warrior chiefs such as Seet Mati in Baddibu. As a result of frequent raids carried out from his territory, an expedition was organized against him in 1890. Ali Bouri fled, and Samba Laube Penda was elected in his place.

History of the Southern Zone (Sine-Salum)[22]

The country was according to tradition settled by Serer under Samba Sar who came from the region of Jolof and settled at Diognick where he founded the village of Djilor. Soon afterwards the area was invaded by the *gelowar*, who were said to be Mandinka[23] of the Mane clan from Kabu. The *gelowar* were a nobility said to possess supernatural powers, and tracing descent matrilineally. The child of a

[15] De la Courbe, 1685, p. 132; Le Maire, 1682 (Ed. of 1887), pp. 48–9.
[16] Barbot, 1732, p. 425.
[17] Durand, 1806, pp. 148–9; Labat, 1828, IV, pp. 131, etc.
[18] Saugnier, 1791, p. 189.
[19] Golberry, 1802, p. 104; Mollien, 1818, p. 54.
[20] Park, 1797, pp. 341-2.
[21] Boilat, 1853, p. 43.
[22] The first four paragraphs are based largely on Le Mire, 1946.
[23] Hecquard, 1855, however, in his account of Kabu considers that the *gelowar* were originally Wolof!

THE WOLOF OF SENEGAMBIA

gelowar mother was always a *gelowar*. They settled first at Coular (Kular) and spread gradually over Sine-Salum.

Salum split into a series of minor chieftainships, after an attempt by a son of the *Burba Jɔlɔf* to seize power in Salum by murdering the *Bur Salum*. Salum Suware had established himself as a chief around Kahone, and was succeeded by his nephew (presumably his sister's son) Eliman Musa, a Tukulor. The ruler of Sine raised an army against him, and defeated the Tukulors. Djilor was torn by civil war over the succession to the position of Mbur-Djilor, and from this time on the centre of power passed to Kahone.

In 1862 Ama Ba (Mabah, Hamah Bah, Amady Ba, Ma Ba Tiakha), a Tukulor marabout, began a holy war, first defeating the *Bur Sine*. He then formed an alliance with the ex-*Damεl* of Kayor (Macodou) and defeated the *Bur Salum* (Samba Laube Fal). The ex-*Damεl* did not live to enjoy his victory, dying—some say poisoned—in 1863, while Samba Laube died the following year, leaving Ama Ba master of Salum. Subsequently the Serer of the Djilor region were massacred in a series of expeditions, though the Nyominka of the islands retained their independence. Towards the end of 1864 the French entered into a treaty with Ama Ba whereby he was recognized as chief of Baddibu and Salum " qu'il gouverna sous le nom d'Almany," and by which he was bound to respect neighbouring territories. However, he began a series of raids into Baol (1865), Jolof, and even as far as the borders of Kayor. About this time he also tried to establish an alliance with the Tukulors of Futa and the Mauretanians, and to create a vast anti-French Muslim confederation. He returned to Rip, where he was defeated by the French expedition of 1866, this campaign breaking his alliance with the Tukulors and Mauretanians. But in 1867 he resumed his raids on Nyomi and Salum, and later Sine and Baol. A small French contingent opposing him was defeated, but the delay caused by the fighting gave the *Bur Sine* time to organize his forces and Ama Ba was forced to retreat. In a second invasion the *Bur Sine* (Kumba Ndofan Juf) was well prepared, and Ama Ba was killed at Marout near Kaolack in July 1867.

The people of Salum recovered, chose another *Bur*, Nyaut Mboj, who began war on Ama Ba's brother and successor Mamud Nderi Ba. There then followed several *Bur Salum* in quick succession.

Mamud Nderi Ba was recognized by the British as chief of Baddibu, but civil war soon broke out (1877) from a revolt of one of Ama Ba's generals (Biram Sise), who had established a sphere of influence at Samba Yasin, not far north of Ker Katim, and made himself independent. In 1884 Ama Ba's son, Seet Mati Ba,[24] had become strong enough to claim the chieftainship from Mamud Nderi, and in a couple of years had assumed control over most of the country. He continued the war against Biram Sise, but through the intervention of the British Acting Administrator peace was established in 1887.

Seet Mati, however, decided to wage war against the Serer and formed an alliance with Jolof against them. Gedel Mboj, the *Bur Salum*, obtained help from the French and Seet Mati was defeated at Kumbof (Goumboff). He fled for refuge to Albreda in the Gambia, crossed to Bathurst, and finished his days in exile at Bakau. Gedel Mboj then became *Bur* of all Salum.

The *Bur Sine* had placed his country under French Protection in 1877, and in 1891 treaties were made with both Sine and Salum by which they were placed under French Protection and administered by them.

The Anglo-French boundary cut off part of Salum, Upper Salum in British Gambia, roughly corresponding to the old district of Pakala. The rulers of Pakala, known as *Seriny Pakala*, were installed by and owed allegiance to the *Bur Kahone*, but as their district was predominantly Muslim they took the side of Ama Ba. After his death they became subjects of his successors, Mamud Nderi and Seet Mati, but the leading warriors (*saltige*) were in fact more concerned with establishing

---

[24] Sait Mati Ba, Saide Mattie, etc.

HISTORY AND TRADITIONS OF ORIGIN

minor chieftainships of their own than with the success of Seet Mati. In the struggle between Biram Sise and Seet Mati allegiance was divided, some villages supporting one, some the other.

In pre-protectorate days the position of *Seriny Pakala* rotated among the leading men of a group of related villages (Bati Hai, Makagui, Panchang, and Maka Andalla), the last ruler being Manjok Sise of Bati Hai. He and his followers (*saltige*) had fought on the side of Seet Mati, but after his defeat had switched allegiance back to the *Bur Kahone*. When the Anglo-French boundary was established, Pakala was still under Manjok Sise. He chose to remain on the French side of the boundary at Nganda, and when called to meet the Governor at Kau-ur, fearing that he might be arrested or punished, sent Sawalo Sise, one of the leading *saltige*, to say that he was his representative. Sawalo Sise was appointed first chief (*sɛf*) under the British, another potential candidate from Bati apparently having declined the position.

LANGUAGE

The Wolof language, classified by Westermann and Bryan (1952) as a West Atlantic Language Larger Unit, is spoken throughout the Senegal, in Jolof, Walo, Kayor, Baol, and Sine-Salum. It is the commercial language of the area and is consequently commonly spoken in trade centres outside this area in the Casamance, Sudan, etc., by Lebanese, Mauretanians, and Moroccans.

Angrand (1943) states that Wolof is the mother tongue of more than a million people and the additional tongue of more than 500,000. De Tressan (1953) gives the number of speakers in French territory as 840,000, including Lebu. These figures may well be exaggerated.

De Tressan[1] has provided a detailed list of the cantons in the Senegal in which Wolof is spoken. In the Gambia, Wolof is spoken in Bathurst, in the Salum districts, and the adjacent areas of Sabah, Sanjal, and Niani; in parts of Nyomi and Niamina, as well as in the trade centres. The language is known as *wɔlɔf* in Bathurst, and *ɔlɔf* in Salum, though educated people in Bathurst, when speaking English, often call it *jɔlɔf*. *Jɔlɔf*, however, is properly the name of the area from which Wolof domination spread in the Senegambian region.

There are regional variations in spoken Wolof, the forms spoken in St. Louis, Dakar, Bathurst, Salum, etc., being distinguished by differences in elisions and contractions, plosion and non-plosion of final p, t, k, and c, and phrases and expressions characteristic of certain areas.

Wolof has been seriously studied since the beginning of the last century, by Dard (1815–20); by Baron Roger, Governor of the Senegal, about the same period; and by the Abbé Boilat, about 1850, but it was chiefly through the influence of Mgr. Kobès, the second Apostolic Vicar of the Senegambia (1847–72), and under his direction, that most work—the compilation of dictionaries and the translation of religious works—was undertaken. In England the study of Wolof was begun in 1820 by Mrs. Kilham. Two Africans, a Wolof and a Mandinka, knowing only a little pidgin English, were selected from a ship arriving in England and, with their assistance, she began studying the languages and preparing elementary school books.

Though a large number of works has been produced,[2] there is still little that is of practical use to anyone wishing to learn the language at the present day. The best Wolof dictionaries, though somewhat old, are still Mgr. Kobès' *Dictionnaire Volof-Français* and le R. P. V.-J. Guy-Grand *Dictionnaire Français-Volof*, both revised by le R. P. O. Abiven (1923). The latter is preceded by a useful summary of Wolof grammar. The only phonetic study of Wolof that has been made is Dr. Ida Ward's short account of Wolof as spoken in Bathurst and the Senegal.

The spelling of Wolof is in an extremely confused state, as can be seen from the scripts used by various authors.

FRENCH SOURCES				ENGLISH SOURCES			
			French popular spelling	*Wesleyan Prayer Book*	*Bible translation*	*Ward*	*Convention adopted in this study*
Kobès	*Labouret*	*Angrand*					
d̤ [3]	d'	di / dj	dj	j	j	j	j
h	ẋ	kh	kh	*h*	ḥ	x	h
ñ	n'	ni) / gn	gne	*n*	ñ	ny	ny
t̤ [3]	t'	tch / thi	thi	*c*	ch	c	ch
v	w	w / ou	v / ou	w	w	w	w
g	g	gu	gu	g	g	g	g

[1] De Tressan, pp. 146–50.
[2] See bibliography, pp. 81–3.
[3] Owing to printing difficulties a single dot has been used for the two found in the original script.

LANGUAGE

In writing vowel sounds use has been made of acute, grave, and circumflex accents, and the umlaut, lines to indicate length, italics, etc.

The Wolof of the Gambia state that those of the Senegal speak Wolof with French tones and accents, while those in Senegal say that the people of Bathurst talk Wolof as if it were English. Wolof as spoken in Salum is very close to that gives in Kobès' dictionary. Bathurst Wolof shows a greater divergence owing to the adoption of many European words, especially from French, and modification of some of the gutteral sounds. An initial *h* found in Salum is absent in Bathurst, e.g., *ñɛn* in Salum, *ɛn* in Bathurst—a load.

The main characteristics of the language are:—

(a) It is not a tone language like Ibo or Twi, but one with strong and weak stresses.

(b) Word roots are generally consonant-vowel-consonant (CVC), or CVC with an unstressed final vowel (in southern Wolof), contrasting with its neighbour Mandinka with a CV-CV pattern.

(c) There are a large number of diphthongs (see Ward), which makes the writing of Wolof difficult with conventional script.

(d) Vowel length is significant: e.g., *lal*, bed; *laal*, to touch; *gis naa ko*, I saw it; *gis na ko*, he saw it.

(e) The initial consonant of the determinative particle is variable (*b, g, j, k, m, s, w, l, ny*, and *y*), sometimes agreeing with the initial letter of the noun (e.g., *mus mi*, the cat; *jigɛn ji*, the woman), sometimes indicating a general class (*j* is used for words indicating a relationship, and for most Arabic words: *g* for trees, *b* for nouns referring to persons, and with most borrowed words, etc.). The present-day tendency is for *b* to be used more and more in everyday speech to the exclusion of other forms. The degree of determination or proximity is indicated by change in the vowel: *i*, near; *a*, far away; *u*, indeterminate.

(f) The verbal root can be modified by many suffixes: e.g., *ab*, to borrow; *abal*, to lend; *abat*, to borrow again; *abati*, to go to borrow again; *abkat*, borrower, etc. Guy-Grand lists over 30 suffixes.

No adequate studies of the Wolof verbal system have yet been made, though the early grammarians provide examples of an enormous number of Wolof "tenses." Thirty-eight affirmative voice and 38 negative voice forms are given by Guy-Grand.

The essential characteristics of the system are as follows: the root remains constant, and subsidiary words which often combine with the pronouns in a contracted form indicate time or the type of action. In general there is a distinction between action on the one hand, and states and explanations on the other. Continuous action in the present or immediate future is shown by the pronoun + *ng* + a vowel + the radical. *Mangi fi*, "I am here"; *mange dɛm*, "I am going";[4] *manga dɛm*, "I am going (far)."[5] *Da* is used in describing generalized actions not being performed at the moment of speaking, "I am writing a new book," or states, *da ma febar*, "I am sick." Definite action in the future is indicated by *di; di naa dɛm*, "I will go, I must go." Past action which still has an effect in the present, e.g., "He has gone" (and is still away) is indicated by the radical followed by the pronoun (combining with *na*) *dɛm na*, "He has gone." This form is also used for verbs such as *ham*, to know; *dega*, to hear, etc.; *ham nga?* "Do you know?" Action over and done with is marked by the suffix (*w*)*ɔn*, roughly corresponding to the English "did," and is used especially in questions and answers. Habitual action is shown by *dan*, followed by the pronoun and radical; incompleted (interrupted) action by *dɔn; fo dɔn dɛm?* "Where were you going?", "Where would you have gone?"; conditional ("I would have gone") by *kɔn*.

---

[4] This could also be translated "Here I am going."

[5] *i* indicates proximity, *a* distance, *e* a case of vowel harmony.

24   THE WOLOF OF SENEGAMBIA

Negatives are shown by the addition of *u, ul* (*ut* in some dialects). *Dɛmu ma,* " I did not go "; *du ma dɛm,* " I will not go "; *da ma febarul,* " I am not sick." Modifications are made to the pronouns to produce stressed forms, both subjective " It is he who did it " *mo* (presumably from *mu la*) *ko dɛf,* and objective " It is you I am talking to " *you laa* (from *la ma?*) *wah.* Various combinations of these elements can be made.

Neku ma fi wɔn.—I was not there (then).

Da ma dɛm ɔn.—I had gone.

You laa dan gis.—It is you I used to see.

The exact relationship between Wolof and neighbouring languages is still difficult to determine with the present lack of reliable analyses of the languages and dialects of this area, particularly of the Serer group. An extreme viewpoint is taken by Angrand, who states, " Elle ne resemble à aucun des idiomes des peuples avoisinant leurs pays." Cheikh Anta Diop considers that there is a close resemblance both in vocabulary and syntax between Keguem Serer and Wolof, though it is probable that many words given as Wolof are borrowings from Serer with a rather limited distribution, the result of Wolof infiltration into a Serer area. Diop (1948) claims to find similarities in a number of Serahuli and Wolof words, but in his examples there is confusion between roots and suffixes, the roots in Wolof finding their similarity in the Serahuli suffix! Structurally Serahuli belongs to the Mandinka-Bambara group, and a high proportion of the words common to Wolof and Serahuli are those connected with trade or trade goods (Serahuli borrowing from Wolof), or groundnut farming (Wolof borrowing from Sudanic migrant farmers).

From Arabic Wolof has acquired a large vocabulary relating to the Islamic religion, incantations, law and certain moral ideas, Arabic writing, the calendar, terms of salutation, camels, horses and their harness; from French the names of objects manufactured in Europe; from Mandinka the names of garden products, of things connected with rice farming, and the names of trees whose natural habitat is south of the Wolof zone; from European sources (French, English, and Portuguese), the names of introduced fruits.

LITERATURE

Proverbs

Among the Wolof verbal wit and a clever tongue are highly esteemed.[6] Dard (1826), in his *Grammaire Wolofe,* gives a list of 231 proverbs with a French translation. An English version of this appears in Burton's *Wit and Wisdom from West Africa* (1865). Some are to be found in Boilat (1856), Roger (1829), and the *Guide de la conversation Français-Volof.* Later writers—Bérenger-Féraud (1879), Delafosse (1922), Angrand (1943), etc.—repeat these. Numerous examples are scattered throughout Kobès' Wolof-French dictionary. Typical are:—

When a mouse makes fun of a cat, there is a hole.

The frog likes water, but not boiling water.

An insolent tongue is a bad weapon.

What a child says, it has heard at home.

If the dog is not at home, it does not bark.

A woman who loses a rival has no grief.

Riddles

The Wolof have a vast repertoire of riddles, though few have been published. Some are to be found in Boilat and in Roger and are repeated by Bérenger-Féraud and Angrand.

[6] Sadji introducing some Wolof proverbs in his novel *Nini* writes: " Gens spirituels jusqu'au cynisme, ils condensent leurs jugements en des formules qui passent de la bouche des grands à celles des jeunes générations. Kott-Barma (i.e., Kɔche Barma, see p. 26) demeure légendaire par les multiples sentences qu'il a laissées après lui . . ."

LANGUAGE   **25**

What has a tail but does not move it?—A ladle.
What breathes but does not live?—Bellows.
What teaches without speaking?—A book.
Three children of the same mother, who are together, but cannot touch one another?—The three feet of an iron pot.
There is a group intermediate between riddles and proverbs:—
Three things essential in this world.—Friends, a good appearance, and bags of money.
The three best things in the world.—Health, to be on good terms with one's neighbours, and to be loved by all.
Three things irresistable in combination.—Woman, the king, and the devil.

Secret Languages

In common with the Mandinka, Serahuli, Fulbe, etc., the Wolof have secret languages. Two types can be distinguished, one used by the *gewɛl*[7] who have special words known only to them, and a second formed by the transposition of consonants or syllables, e.g., *mai ma ndɔh*, give me water, becomes *ma mai ɔh ndo,* This latter type is generally used by boys. A further modification can be made with the addition of letters or syllables. Boys often learn these secret languages during the period of seclusion following circumcision, or from their companions at the *dara* (Arabic school).

Some details of the secret languages are given by Labouret in *Les Pêcheurs de Guet N'Dar* (1934). A description of the secret languages of the Fulbe, which also mentions that of the Wolof, is given by Gaden (1914). A brief note is also provided by Mademba Gaye (1944).

Stories

The Wolof have a vast fund of stories. Most are animal tales in which the chief characters are generally the hyaena and the hare (the cunning hare normally getting the better of the hyaena who is depicted as deceitful but rather stupid), but tales are also told of lion, goat, ass, monkey, cock, and dog. Some have human characters and deal with such themes as jealousy between wives, the problems of childless wives, and the eventual punishment of wrongdoers.

There are also narratives which belong to Islamic tradition relating the deeds of the prophets, Noah, Moses, Solomon, Mohammed, etc.

Comparatively few stories seem to have been published, perhaps because most Wolof stories have a Rabelaisian touch which prevents their characteristic style appearing in sober print. French translations of Wolof stories are given by Equilbecq (1915), Cendrars (1947), Ousmane Soce (1942), and Bérenger-Féraud (1885); about 20 stories by Sadji are included in René Guillot's *Contes d'Afrique* (1933). A school reading book by Senghor and Sadji (1953) is based on the tales of Leuk the hare. De la Courbe gives the tale of the three sons of Noah and this is repeated by Labat and Bérenger-Féraud.

Only a very few Wolof texts have been published. A story of the monkey and the hare—the hare which could not keep still and the monkey which could not refrain from scratching—is given by Boilat. That of the hyaena—which fell down a well, was pulled out by a cow and then wished to devour her—is found in the *Guide de la conversation Français-Volof.* The tales of the hare and the sparrows, the grub and the butterfly, the wolf and the spirit of death are recorded by Boilat.

Legends, History, etc.

The *gewɛl* recite genealogies, telling the length of the reigns of kings and chiefs, and their actions on the field of battle, as well as recounting tales of famous

[7] See p. 45.

THE WOLOF OF SENEGAMBIA

warriors. There are *gewɛl* lineages attached to each of the major " clans," whose history they are expected to know, e.g., in Salum the Jɛngs are the *gewɛl* of the Sises.

A few narratives have appeared in the writings of European authors. The story of the war between the *Damɛl* of Kayor and the Almani Abdulkader of Futa Toro, and the *Damɛl's* treatment of his defeated adversary is related by Mungo Park, while accounts of Wolof who preferred death to dishonour in war will be found in Mollien.[8]

The most famous among the classic stories of Wolof oral literature are the tales of the philosopher Kɔche Barma[9] which are given by Rousseau[10] in his analysis of the " Cahiers de Yoro Dyao." The story of Kɔche and the four tufts of hair which he left on his son's head is also related by Boilat, Bérenger-Féraud and Angrand.

Each tuft, said Kɔche, represented a true saying known only to himself and his wife. The first, " A king is neither a relative nor a friend "; the second, " A stepson is not a son, but a civil war "; the third, " One should love one's wife, but not entrust her with one's secrets "; the fourth, " An old man is essential in a country." Kɔche was betrayed by his wife, who told the king the secret she shared with him. The king condemned Kɔche to death for his first statement, in spite of his long and numerous services. His stepson tried to take away his garments before he was executed, saying that he was due to inherit them, and that they ought not to be soiled by his blood, but, at the very last moment, an old man intervened and obtained a pardon for Kɔche, thus confirming the truth of the statements.

Songs

Translations of some of the songs of the *gewɛl* are given by Reade; of the songs of women affected by trances by Balandier; of phrases from the songs of newly circumcised boys by A. G. Thiam.

The Wolof texts of songs in honour of particular people, of war songs and of satirical songs are given by Boilat. Examples of songs sung in children's games and lullabies are to be found in Béart.

Religious Literature

Some Bible stories in Wolof appear in Dard's *Grammaire Wolofe*. The Gospels of St. Matthew and St. John have been published in Wolof, the translation having been made by the Wesleyan Mission in Bathurst. The Mission also published a catechism (date uncertain); a primer by Fieldhouse, which included translations of the Beatitudes, the Ten Commandments, the Creed, and the Lord's Prayer; a religious reading book (1909); and a book of 50 hymns (1909). These four books are now generally unobtainable.

The Roman Catholic Missions, especially the Mission of Saint-Joseph de N'Gazobil (Ngasobil) have translated a considerable amount of material—catechisms, Bible stories, hymns, etc. A list of these is given in the bibliography.

The Islamic sects—the Tijaniya, the Mourides, etc., have produced both hymns and commentaries on Arabic texts.

School Books

The first school books in Wolof were prepared by Mrs. Kilham in 1820–23,[11] with the assistance of two Africans who were taught to read and write in England. The first book was planned so that the pupil could begin learning the alphabet in groups of six letters, practising reading and writing on monosyllables, then on to

[8] 1820, pp. 53–4.
[9] Kothe in Yoro Dyao; Cotche in Angrand; Cothi in Bérenger-Féraud.
[10] Rousseau, 1941–2, p. 105.
[11] See linguistic bibliography, p. 81.

single words, and finally to short sentences. The second was a larger and much improved work, designed to lead to the acquisition of English at an early stage. Typically 19th-century instructional tales for children were given, Wolof on one page, English on the opposite page. Part II of the work consisted of good moral advice for elders (English and Wolof), and a Wolof-English vocabulary; Part III, a selection of Biblical extracts with their translations. She later prepared reading cards in 30 African languages including Wolof, Fula, and Mandinka.

PHYSICAL ENVIRONMENT

CLIMATE

Seasons

Feb.-May: The hot season. No rain. A hot east wind blowing, drying the soil, and withering vegetation.

June: First rains. Characterized by tornadoes due to the meeting of the monsoons and the east wind, causing whirlwinds and storms. Considerable dust storms may be raised before the rain, which often comes in short, violent thunderstorms.

July-Sept.: The rainy season.

October: End of the rains. Very humid conditions. Rains terminate with further violent storms.

Nov.-Jan.: The temperature falls gradually. The north wind begins to blow, while a dry sea breeze is felt in the coastal zone. Sometimes high clouds give a little rain. The sky becomes dull and hazy.

Rainfall

The Wolof zone covers a wide range of rainfall, from about 330 mm. (13 ins.) in the north to over 1,000 mm. (40 ins.) in the south, the rainfall also being very variable from year to year. In the north the rains fall from July to October, while in the south they begin earlier (June) and end later (November), and the number of rainy days is greater.

Average rainfall figures are:—

	mm.	*Years*	*Source*
Podor	333	1931–40	Papy
Dagana	360	1931–40	,,
St. Louis	380	1921–48	Brasseur
Bakel	510	1921–48	,,
Dakar	546	1921–48	,,
Fatick	800	1921–48	,,

VEGETATION[1]

As the rainfall of the Wolof zone varies so greatly from north to south, the vegetation also ranges almost from rain forest to desert. The proximity of the sea increases the humidity and modifies the temperature and flora of the coastal region which is bordered by a chain of sand dunes behind which is the region of the " Niayes ", a sandy plain, with heavier soil in places and a series of swamps of fresh or slightly salty water on the edge of which one finds vegetation of the rain forest type, with oil palms (*tir*), Khaya senegalensis (*hai*), etc. Mangroves border the mouths of rivers.

Inland, on the lighter and sandier soils, the characteristic trees are *wɔlo* (Terminalia sp.), *nɛtɛ* (Parkia biglobosa), *dimba* (Cordyla africana), *beit* (Scelerocarya Birrea), *soto* (Ficus sp.), *ninkom* (Spondias Monbin), *son* (Lannea sp.), *ndakhar* or *dahar* (Tamarindus indica), *faftan* (Calotropis procera), *nɛb-nɛb* or *nɛp-nɛp* (Acacia arabica), *rat* (Combretum sp.), *sibi* (Borassus æthiopum), *alom* (Diospyrus mespiliformis), *kada* (Acacia albida), *sedɛm* or *dɛm* (Ziziphus jujuba), *sɔlɔm* (Dialium guineense), *neou* (Parinari macrophylla) and, *ditah* (Detarium senegalense). On the poorer soils of laterite ridges one may find various acacias, e.g., *dɛda* (Acacia macrostachya), *wɔlɔ* (Terminalia avicennioides) *kindindɔlo* (Combretum Lecardii), etc. On the borders of swamps *xɔs* or *hɔs* (Mitragyna inermis), *ngigis* (Bauhinia Thonningii), *seb* (Phœnix reclinata); round villages the baobab, *gui* (Adansonia digitata), and *bɛntɛnki* (Ceiba pentandra), the cotton tree.

---

[1] For the vegetation of Senegal consult J. Trochain: *Contribution à l'étude de la végétation du Sénégal*, MEM. IFAN, No. 2, 1940. A large number of Wolof names of plants are given in J. M. Dalziel: *The useful plants of West Tropical Africa*. See also le R. P. Sébire: *Plantes utiles du Sénégal* (1895).

ECONOMY

CROPS

The Wolof grow bulrush millet[1] and sorghum (*dugub, dugup*) and groundnuts (*gɛrtɛ*) and plant relatively little rice (*malo*), though in some of the southern zones, owing to pressure of population, the exhaustion of upland soils, and the influence of neighbouring Mandinka peoples, rice growing is important in their economy. Digitaria (*findi*)[2] is very rarely planted. Maize (*mbɔha*) is sown in the compounds and back gardens. An early ripening millet (*suna*) is grown in plots round the compounds where it can be guarded against birds when ripening. Cotton (*witɛn*) is often interplanted with the *suna*. More *suna* is grown in the northern zone than in the south.

In Salum only a small quantity of *sanyo* (a bulrush millet with rough hairs which birds dislike) is grown, and the main crop is a sorghum (*wɛndi*), generally called *basi* in local speech. The large-grained *basi* (*basi bu rei*) is planted in only a few villages. Some coarse large-grained sorghum with a dependent head (*fela*)[3] is grown for feeding to livestock.

Numerous minor crops are grown—beans (*nyɛbe* or *seb*), often interplanted with sorghum after the first weeding; sorrel (*basab*,Hibiscus sabdariffa) and garden eggs (*batanse*)[4] on farm boundaries (generally by women); tomatoes (*mɛntɛŋ*), red peppers (*kani*), okra (*kanja*),[5] and bitter tomato (*jahatu*) in the plots behind the houses. Beniseed (*bene*) is sometimes seen, though this was commoner in former times. Some native tobacco plants (*tamaka*) may be found under the house eaves, whence they are transplanted later to open sites in the compound. Gourds (*yɔmba*) and pumpkins (*banga*) trail along the fences and over the roofs, and large gourds used for calabashes (*lɛkɛt*) are grown out on the farms. Few root crops are planted, some sweet potatoes (*patas* or *patat*), a little cassava (*nyambi*), and sometimes aereal yams[6] (Dioscorea sp.). *Pɔndɔre* (Hibiscus cannabinus), the fibres of which are used in making tie-tie, is also grown in the backyards. Bambara groundnuts (*nyɛbe-gɛrtɛ*)[7] and indigo (*nganja*) are only rarely grown.

Compared with the Mandinka and Serahuli the Wolof have few fruit trees. Pawpaws and mangos are planted, but oranges and limes find more favourable climatic conditions south of the Wolof zone. The baobab, however, provides the Wolof with fruit, leaves (*lalo*) used as food, and bark which is made into rope.

FARMING METHODS

In clearing farms the Wolof use a locally made narrow bladed iron axe (*semɛny*) and a matchet (*jasi*), generally an imported type. An adze-shaped tool (*kɔnko*) may also be used in chopping bushes. A rake (*sudi*) made of a bamboo pole, the end of which is split into half-a-dozen segments and held apart with a cross stick, is used for clearing. If grass is abundant it is first burnt off by fire; then shrubs, clumps of grass, etc., are piled in heaps and burnt shortly before the rainy season is due to begin.

One of the essential differences between the Wolof and their Mandinka neighbours is that where population density is low, the Wolof are much less destructive of the bush in preparing land for farming. Along the edges of the swamps millet is planted in among the rhun palms, which are left undisturbed, only the

---

[1] Henceforth the term millet is used to include both sorghum and bulrush millet.
[2] *Fonyo* in the language of the Fulbe.
[3] Known as *Bambarang baso* in Mandinka.
[4] i.e., Brinjal, egg plant, aubergine.
[5] i.e., Gombo. Hibiscus esculentus.
[6] In Salum this is known as *wusu*, but it is not to be confused with the *wusu* of the Mandinka and Serahuli which is a small tuber 5 cms. long with a black skin tasting like boiled potato. (Coleus sp.?)
[7] Voandzeia subterranea (Pois souterrains).

debris on the ground being burnt. When bush is cleared, tree stumps 3 to 4 ft. high are left. This means that when a farm is left to rest or abandoned, the vegetation grows up quickly, helping to restore the fertility of the soil. This process is helped by the greater mobility of the Wolof.

Villages are abandoned, and new ones founded; migration takes place from villages that have become large, with the result that periodically large tracts of farmland are temporarily abandoned and revert to secondary bush. On the other hand vegetation near the older Wolof villages is as thoroughly cleared as among the Mandinka.

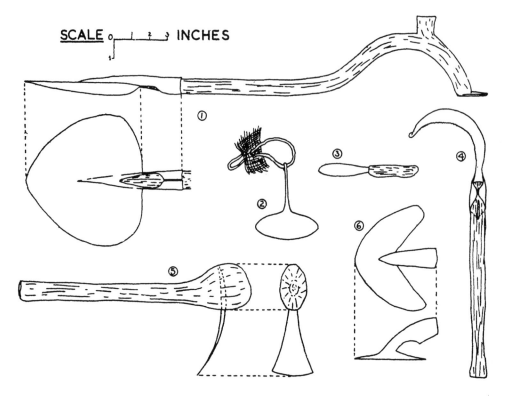

1. The instrument known as *iler* in Salum, its handle as *sɔh-sɔh*.
2. The *ngoban,* a knife for harvesting millet.
3. Rice cutting knife.
4. Sickle (locally made).
5. The *kɔnko,* used in planting groundnuts.
6. The blade of the tool called *jahai* in Salum, *iler* in Kayor.

While Mandinka and Jola plant their groundnuts on ridges, the Wolof plant on the flat. They begin to clear their farms early in the year, taking advantage of the first heavy rain for extensive and rapid planting. For sowing groundnuts they have adopted from the Serahuli or Mandinka an adze-shaped tool (*kɔnko*) which is held in one hand and used to make a series of holes in the ground, the seed being dropped in with the other hand. The earth is pressed down over the holes with the feet as the sower moves along. For millet planting a long-handled pole over 6 ft. long tipped with an iron blade (*daba*) is used to make a series of shallow holes. The sowers follow behind, dropping in the seeds which they carry in small calabashes, pushing the soil back into the holes and pressing it down with their feet.

ECONOMY   31

For the Wolof the main work of the farming season consists of a continuous battle against weeds for which they use the *iler*.[8] There is confusion regarding this term, for the Wolof of Salum use it to mean an instrument like an inverted shovel blade, heart-shaped, on a short handle (*sɔh-sɔh*), which is used in a squatting position, the tool being pushed to and fro to loosen a thin layer of soil. Among the Wolof to the north the *iler* is a half-moon shaped blade on a 5 or 6 ft. handle, used in a standing position, the *sɔh-sɔh* being unknown. This crescent-shaped blade the Salum Wolof call *jahai*. It is used sometimes for weeding and clearing, but seems rather to have gone out of fashion, being used now for weeding compounds and village streets rather than for farm work. These tools are illustrated on page 30.

On the groundnut farms, when the plants have spread and the nuts are forming, any necessary weeding has to be carried out by hand to avoid damage to the nuts. When crops are ripening they have to be protected against animals. Baboons and monkeys may pull up groundnuts, but the greatest loss is caused by birds which eat millet, the *suna* in particular having to be guarded from dawn till dusk. High platforms are built on which women and children keep watch, shouting, singing, throwing stones, using slings, and shaking long cords to which tin cans, pieces of cloth, etc., are tied. Scarecrows are also set up in the fields.

When groundnuts are ripe the *iler* is used for loosening the soil so that they can be lifted. They are left for a short period on the ground, then gathered into small heaps like hay cocks to dry for a while, and finally stacked on raised platforms or heaps of brushwood. A pole about 6 ft. long is used for gathering in the small heaps of nuts and piling them on the stack. They are threshed on a hard piece of ground, usually the site of an old ant-hill, beside the groundnut stack. Two sticks, one held in each hand, about the length of walking sticks and with a hook about 6 ins. long at one end, are used to beat the haulms. The hook is held downwards and outwards when beating, and is used to pull down further material from the stack and stir over the pile of haulms. When the haulms have been broken up and the nuts separated from the stalks, they are winnowed by being shaken out of a basket held head high or dropped from the hands, so that the wind can blow away the stalks and dust. They are then put in sacks and taken to trade centres by lorry or donkey.

Rice farming techniques have been derived from the Mandinka. A long-handled hoe with a springy shaft is used in working the ground. Seed beds are first prepared at the beginning of the rainy season, and the rice later transplanted. Certain ritual prohibitions have also been taken over, e.g., women do not work rice farms on Wednesdays. Rice is harvested with a small knife, each head being cut separately.

If *findi* is grown it is harvested with a sickle (*sarta* or *refan*). In harvesting millet the stalks are first flattened by pressing on them with the foot; the heads are then cut with a knife about 4 ins. long and 1½ ins. wide (*ngoban*) held in the palm of the hand between the index finger and the thumb, the stalk of millet being gripped by the fingers and pressed down on the blade. Even when a European knife is used it is still held in the same way. Bulrush millet, if well dry, can easily be broken by the hand. Millet is generally stacked on the head and threshed as required by pounding in a mortar. It is said to keep better on the head, though subject to some damage by rats.

Use is made of cattle[9] for manuring the millet farms round the village where the land is more or less continuously cultivated. At night the animals are tethered

---

[8] Some sources attribute the introduction of the *iler* to Hilaire Maurel of the firm of Maurel and Prom. R. M. and J. R.-M. in a note in *Notes Africaines* point out that Hilaire Maurel did not arrive in Senegal till 1830, whereas the name *hiller* is mentioned in 1821, and was described without being named in 1695. In the vocabularies of Mrs. Kilham hoe is translated *E-la-er* in the book published in 1820, and *I-le-er* in 1823.

[9] See below, p. 33.

THE WOLOF OF SENEGAMBIA

to small stakes driven into the ground, the tethering places being moved from time to time during the dry season so that the whole area surrounding the settlement is manured. Patches of land round the compounds used for maize and *suna* are fertilized by household rubbish.

The Wolof follow a system of rotation of crops, the sequence on a number of Salum farms being:—

	A	B	C	D	E
1948	groundnuts	*sanyo*	groundnuts	*sanyo*	*wɛndi*
1947	*sanyo*	groundnuts	*sanyo & wɛndi*	groundnuts	groundnuts
1946	*wɛndi*	*sanyo*	groundnuts	not farmed	*wɛndi*
1945	groundnuts	groundnuts	*sanyo & suna*		not farmed
1944	*wɛndi*	not cleared	groundnuts		
1943	secondary bush		resting for at least 5 years		

Only in the rhun palm belt or on manured land can millet be cultivated for a number of years in succession without a change. In the richer soil of the rhun palm belt it can often be grown for five years before signs of exhaustion become apparent.

Some mixed cropping is found in Salum. Practically all groundnut farms have rows of millet planted across them at intervals of 6 to 9—or sometimes only 3 to 4—yds., and on many millet farms there is a substantial crop of volunteer (i.e., self-sown) groundnuts. Beans are interplanted with *basi*, cotton with the early ripening *suna*, while in the plots in and near the compounds there is a mixture of all the minor crops—tomatoes, peppers, okra, bitter tomato, cassava, sweet potatoes, etc.

As a rule no dry season gardening is carried out.

Though the Wolof have a high degree of skill and empirical knowledge and a good appreciation of the potentialities of various soils, their farming must still be considered primitive, and the export groundnut crop has been developed at the expense of a progressive deterioration of the soils, and of woodland degeneration, brought about by the use of fires for clearing and over-cultivation. Improvements are now being made by the introduction of selected lines of seed nuts which give larger yields, experiments with artificial fertilizers, and irrigation schemes for rice.

AGRICULTURE IN THE NORTHERN ZONE

A system of agriculture based on natural flooding is practised in the Senegal valley. Here large stretches of land are inundated each year and covered with a fertilizing mud. These zones, known as " *oualo,*" are planted with millet, maize, beans, and tobacco as the floods recede and ripen from February to June. The uplands, " *dieri,*" which have a sandy soil, are cultivated during the rainy season, a quick ripening millet which ripens in November being planted.

This system of agriculture appears to be very ancient. At any rate in Marmol (16th century, p. 33) we find such remarks as " they sow the millet in July and harvest it in September because it rains heavily at that time . . . the water from the river is sufficient to make grow what is sown in the low lying land " . . . "they raise the soil fairly lightly in front of them and throw therein their seed, which the floods make abundantly fruitful," while later (p. 75) he describes the method of sowing seed in the mud by covering it with sand so that the plant can break through more easily when the surface dries hard.

ECONOMY   **33**

FARMING CALENDAR, 1950, IN SALUM

Month.		Rainfall* (inches)	Agricultural activities.	Other activities.
Apr.	DRY	—	Clearing farms	Dyeing cloth Communal fishing
May		0·460	Distribution of seed groundnuts Burning grass on farms Clearing rice fields	Thatching, house- building
Jun.	RAINS	3·850†	Planting maize Planting *suna* Planting millet Planting groundnuts Planting rice	
Jul.		9·475	Planting groundnuts Re-planting millet Planting cassava Weeding	
Aug.		16·870	Weeding Guarding *suna* Transplanting rice	
Sept.		16·915	Guarding farms First *suna* ripe Harvesting maize Volunteer (self sown) groundnuts ripe Transplanting rice	
Oct.		9·470	Digging groundnuts Stacking groundnuts First rice available	Wrestling starts
Nov.		1·295	Harvesting millet Harvesting rice Carrying home crops	
Dec.	DRY	—	Threshing groundnuts Selling groundnuts Completion of rice harvest	
Jan.		—	Picking cotton Selling groundnuts Digging cassava	Marriages negotiated
Feb.		—	Picking cotton	Spinning cotton Transfer of brides
Mar.		—	Gleaning nuts	Communal fishing Weaving

58·335

* Data recorded at Keneba in Western Kiang. Rainfall was exceptionally heavy this year.
† There was a drought in June, only 0.660 in. falling from the 12th to the 30th, during which a plague of caterpillars damaged some of the crops, necessitating re-planting.
Quite a useful agricultural calendar is to be found in the Bulletin of IFAN for Juil-Oct., 1940. (See Bibliography under Anon.)

LIVESTOCK

The Wolof have clearly many fewer cattle than the Fulbe, though no exact figures are available, the results of counts or estimates of livestock being prepared by regions without indicating tribal differences. In contrast to the Serer, Jola,[10]

[10] There is a tendency nowadays for Fulbe to take over the work of herding in Fonyi (Jola country).

C

and Serahuli, the Wolof do not as a rule herd cattle themselves. Where a Wolof has acquired a large herd, it is normally looked after by a Fula herdsman; if a Wolof herdsman is employed, he is often found to be of slave descent, and ultimately of Fula origin. When only one or two head of cattle are owned, they are incorporated in a larger herd, often that of a nearby Fula settlement.

The commonest breed in the south is the *ndama* (West African shorthorn). Very occasionally one sees the dwarf Futa Jallon breed. The *gobra* (humped variety) is found to the north, the 14th parallel marking the change.

In the dry season herds move from the inland districts to graze on the flats near the rivers and fresh water streams. During this time they are generally kraaled on the lands round nearby villages at night, Wolof farmers paying the Fulbe for this service. At the beginning of the rains, when fresh grasses sprout, and the trees bear new leaves, the herds return inland to uncultivated bush. At harvest-time they are brought back to graze on millet leaves and groundnut haulms. The movements of cattle depend on availability of water supplies and grazing in the dry season, and pressure on land during the farming season, for if practically all available land is being cultivated the cattle have to be moved away from the area to avoid damaging crops, whereas if density is low, they can still be kept near their home village.

Wolof value their cattle for the milk and manure they provide, and as a reserve of wealth, but there is none of the mystical association between men and cattle that characterizes the Fulbe.

Few sheep are to be seen, though sometimes the large Senegal sheep (Sahel sheep) are bought from Mauretanians to be killed at festivals. Goats are plentiful, and are owned by both men and women. The general practice is for men to buy these for their wives, who look after them. When kids are born the wife keeps the females for herself, while the husband gets the males, which are later either killed and eaten or sold. Women also buy livestock with money from their groundnut farms. During the dry season the goats roam about loose; in the farming period they are taken out by their owners and tethered to pegs or trees, or kept in herds looked after by small boys. Scraggy-looking chickens live in the compounds. They feed on insects and scraps of grain which fly from the mortar during pounding, and at night are shut up in small round fowl houses. Some dogs and an occasional cat are kept. Horses are rarer to-day than formerly, and donkeys are comparatively few in number, motor transport having largely taken their place.

Organization and Division of Labour

Most of the food is produced by the men, who plant the millet. Where rice is grown it is planted by women. Nevertheless, there is a greater degree of co-operation between the sexes than among the Mandinka. On the millet farms a woman may help her husband with the sowing, or remove bundles of weeds from the farm. The greatest share of the work of scaring birds from the maize and *suna* also falls on the young women and girls. Cotton is planted by men, but picked by women. In the rice fields men help to clear heavy grass, carry bundles of rice for transplanting, and guard the fields at night to scare off hippo. Women generally look after the minor crops. When groundnuts are being threshed, they help in the winnowing.

Whereas among the Jola of Fonyi and the Mandinka of the lower Gambia the women do not plant groundnuts, Wolof women and girls have small groundnut plots of their own. Some of the nuts are used for food; the rest are sold to buy ornaments, dresses, etc., or to invest in livestock. Small boys aged from 12 onwards can have groundnut farms if they wish, which they work two days a week, working the rest of the time for their fathers or brothers. Among the Mandinka a man does not have a farm of his own until he is about 18 or 19, while in Fonyi among the Jola a man may still continue working for his father without owning an independent farm even after he is married.

ECONOMY

The Wolof accept considerable numbers of migrant groundnut farmers ("strange farmers" in Gambian English, "navetanes" in West African French), who are often Fulbe, Bambara,[11] or Serahuli. The strange farmer is housed and fed, and in return works on his landlord's farm four days of the week, and on his own farm three days. At the end of the season the strange farmer gives a small present to his landlord, and to the woman who has been cooking for him.

Division of Labour

Men's Work	Women's Work
Clearing farms.	Help guard ripening *suna*.
Millet farming.	Rice farming.
Groundnut farming.	Also have small groundnut plots
Housebuilding.	Help men in winnowing nuts.
Thatching.	Drawing water.
Fencing.	Clothes washing.
Hunting (making traps).	Pounding grain.
Fishing.	Cooking.
Mat-making.	Gathering firewood.
Basket-making.	Cleaning compound.
Weaving.	Looking after children.
Rope-making.	Picking, cleaning, spinning cotton.
Smithing.	Dyeing.
Leatherwork.	Pottery-making.
Butchering.	Hairdressing.
Drumming.	Playing "water drum" (a calabash upturned in a basin of water).
Playing musical instruments.	Care of goats.
Care of cattle.	Gathering leaves, fruits, etc.
Gathering honey.	Harvesting garden products and minor crops.
Large scale trading.	Trading (urban women).
Paddling canoes.	Sale of vegetables in market.
Religious teaching.	Women gather common plants and leaves as medicines.
Doctoring and herbalism.	Midwifery.
Setting fractures.	

LAND TENURE

The rules regarding land tenure vary greatly according to the degree of stability of the population, and the extent of pressure on land. In many Wolof communities mobility is generally such that there is little of the close association between lineages and land that is found, for example, in Mandinka society. A man will clear an area of bush and farm it, his fellow villagers respecting his rights there, but if he leaves the village or abandons the land, it may be taken over by anyone else. In a community with little pressure on land the village head and freeborn elders make their choice of farming land first, then other residents, and finally strangers. A stranger will be taken round by his host and can then choose the land he thinks most suitable. A village head and his elders usually settle any minor disputes within traditional village lands; disputes involving two villages would normally go to the chief for settlement. In areas where population density is high, the patrilineages maintain close rights over land cleared by their ancestors. As a rule the freeborn families control most of the land near the villages, those of slave origin having to farm land farther away in the bush, though they could be given permission to work land not required by its freeborn owners.

---

[11] Fewer Bambara are coming as strange farmers now compared with 20 years ago.

THE WOLOF OF SENEGAMBIA

TRADE

Though the Wolof never had the same reputation for long distance trading as the Serahuli or the Jula branch of the Mandinka, they formerly played an important part in the salt trade with the interior, the early rulers deriving much of their revenue from salt prepared in the coastal region.[12] They also dominated the trade in horses[13] which were obtained from Mauretanians in exchange for slaves, and sold to the Mandinka. Local exchange developed between the coastal region which provided dried fish and oysters and the interior where millet was grown. In the Senegal valley millet was sold both to the Mauretanians and, later, to St. Louis. The main wealth of the Wolof is derived to-day from the groundnut crop, which is their main export. Markets have developed in some of the larger wharf towns and trade centres. A high proportion of the shopkeepers and traders in Senegambia are Wolof. In the dry season pedlars travel round the villages selling such items as head ties, cloth, hats, matches, cigarettes, perfume, powder, ear-rings, slippers, beads, thread, etc. Laube woodworkers bring pestles, mortars, and wooden bowls; the Mauretanians come with cattle. In the villages petty traders sell kola-nuts, cigarettes, tobacco, matches, and a host of miscellaneous wares. From the Gambia there is a considerable export of cotton goods to Wolof territory. In the dry season Wolof women from urban centres go to the grain producing areas to barter palm-oil, dried fish, peppers, salt, kerosene, etc., for rice and millet.

FISHING

A number of fishing methods are in use. During the rainy season weirs are constructed and basket fish traps (*kaia*) set in streams and narrow parts of swamps. In the dry season when the swamps are beginning to dry up and large pools are left, communal fish drives are held in which *segi*—conical baskets open at the bottom, and with a hole at the top through which the fisherman can put his hand—are used. The basket is clamped down over the fish, the fisherman inserts his hand, catches the fish, pulls it out, and threads it on a thin strip of palm leaf tied round his waist. Nets (*sabal*) of various types are used, a common variety being about 5 or 6 ft. long, with sticks attached at each side, which can be closed up like a bag. The coastal Wolof use cast nets and seine nets. Fish are also caught with a barbed spear (*sɔro*) which is thrust in and out of the reeds round the pools where the fish lurk. Coastal fishermen use harpoons with floats attached.

HUNTING

Hunting plays a comparatively small part in Wolof economy. In the dry season, when bush fires spread through the countryside, antelopes and hares are killed. There are a few professional hunters, men covered with amulets designed to ensure that they will meet with game and preserve them from dangers (especially to prevent their ancient Dane guns blowing up). Bows and arrows were used in former days, and though still in use among the Jola and similar peoples south of the Gambia, are merely children's toys with the Wolof. The craft of hunting is subject to numerous ritual observances, and an apprenticeship is served with an experienced hunter to learn the art.

NATURAL PRODUCTS

A host of wild leaves, roots, etc., are used for medicines, magical, and ritual purposes. Balandier[14] lists a number of plants used by the Lebu. Fruits eaten are described in the section *Food*, below. Rhun palm leaves are used for thatching and for weaving into fans and baskets, reeds for fencing and housebuilding. Baobab

---

[12] Jobson, 1620, p. 108.
[13] Moore, 1730, p. 44.
[14] 1952, pp. 99–105.

ECONOMY

bark is twisted into rope, and the leaf dried and used as an ingredient of *chɛrɛ*.[15] The wood of the *dimba* (Cordyla africana) is used for making drums, *bɛntɛnki* (Ceiba pentandra) for canoes, *wɛn* (Pterocarpus erinaceus) for paddles, *ir* (Prosopis africana) for charcoal. The fibre *bakak* (Sansevieria senegambica) is made into wigs for women's hairdressing.

FOOD AND DRINK
Food[16]

The staple food of the Wolof is millet, though those in urban centres consume a large amount of rice. In past years this was imported (polished) rice, an item which had a high snob value, but owing to difficulties in the supply of rice from the Far East, more locally grown rice is now being used.

A variety of minor products are eaten:—

beniseed	*bɛne*	cassava	*nyambi*
beans	*sab, nyɛbe*	sweet potato	*patas*
bitter tomato	*jahatu*	an aereal yam	*wusu* [17]
garden egg (aubergine)	*batanse*		
groundnuts	*gɛrte*	gourd	*yɔmba*
okra	*kanja*	pumpkin	*banga*
onions	*sɔble, linyɔng*		
red peppers	*kani*	locust bean seed	*nɛtetu*
sorrel	*basab*	tamarind	*ndakhar, dahar*
tomatoes	*mɛntɛŋ*,[18] *tamate*	baobab fruit	*bui*
palm-oil	*diu tir*	baobab leaf	*lalo* [19]
groundnut oil	*diwilin*	other leaves	*nebedai*,[20] *mbum ndur,*
butter	*diu nag*		*etc*
fresh milk	*meou*		
sour milk	*sou*		

The main dishes[21] prepared are:—

(A) From millet:

Lah : A porridge of boiled millet, to which sour milk, sugar, and baobab fruit are added. It is generally eaten in the morning. More rarely taken with fresh milk.

Rui : Pap made from granulated millet flour (*karau*), put into boiling water. Eaten in the morning.

Nyelɛŋ :[22] Steamed millet made from coarser grains (*sanhal*) than *chɛrɛ*. Usually eaten for lunch. A soup of groundnuts, tomatoes, peppers, sorrel, locust bean seeds, bitter tomato, etc., and thickened with millet powder (*sunguf*), is taken with it.

Chɛrɛ : Steamed millet flour. Generally eaten at night. Baobab leaf (*lalo*) is added to the millet. The commonest dish with *chɛrɛ* is *base*, made from groundnut paste, peppers, pumpkins or beans and, if available, meat or fish. Sometimes fresh fish alone, or a root crop (cassava or sweet potato) accompanies it. *Chɛrɛ* with milk is sometimes taken for breakfast.

Dabɛrɛ : Millet with a sauce of sorrel (*basab*), groundnuts, and dried fish.

---

[15] See below.
[16] For further details consult Pales: *L'Alimentation en A.O.F.*, 1954.
[17] A name used in Salum. See footnote on p. 29.
[18] *Mɛntɛŋ*—a word borrowed from Mandinka. In Bathurst *tamate* is used primarily for tomato purée and tomato powder.
[19] *Lalo* is a very rich source of calcium.
[20] A perennial plant. From English " Never-die."
[21] The Salum names are given here. The same type of dishes are prepared in Senegal under different names.
[22] From Mandinka *nyelɛŋo*.

THE WOLOF OF SENEGAMBIA

In cooking *chɛre* and *nyelɛŋ* the following method is employed. The flour is put in a clay pot with a perforated bottom set on an iron cooking pot filled with water. The joint is sealed with a paste made from bran and water, and the pot covered with a circular straw cover. After being steamed for a while the millet flour is taken out of the pot with a ladle and put in a calabash. Small amounts are transferred to a basket and shaken to separate the fine flour from the coarser lumps (or it is sifted). The flour is returned to the pot for further steaming. The lumps are put on one side and broken up before being added to the rest. This process is repeated several times. Before the steaming is completed dried and pounded baobab leaf is mixed in.

Subsidiary dishes include: *mbum* made from groundnut sauce and leaves; *datu* from sorrel and usually eaten with *nyelɛŋ; talalɛ* with meat, groundnut oil, and beans.

(B) From rice:

Sɛrɛŋ (Salum):	Groundnuts and locust bean seed pounded and cooked
Mbahal (Bathurst):	with the rice. Peppers, onions, and tomatoes added.
Chura :	A thick porridge of boiled rice; sugar added.
Dɔmoda :	Boiled rice with a stew of groundnuts, onions, peppers, *basab*, okra, tomatoes, etc., with dried fish or meat when available.
Benachin :	Rice, and fish or meat cooked with oil. Onions, tomatoes, peppers, etc., added.
Chu :	Rice, either groundnut- or palm-oil, fowl or meat, onions, tomatoes, sometimes cabbage and macaroni. (An urban dish.)
Supa kanja :	A dish made with okra.

Items which are often sold in markets as snacks include *pankɛt*, pancakes of millet flour; *mbudake—chɛrɛ* with roasted and pounded groundnuts and sugar; fried fish; roasted and boiled groundnuts.

There are not many pawpaw or orange trees in the Wolof area and few of these fruits are eaten, but mangoes are common. Lime juice is often used as an ingredient in cooking. Children eat many wild fruits: *alom, dimba, ditah,*[23] *bui,*[24] *nɛte, neou,*[25] *ninkom, sibi (koka), sedɛm, son.*[26]

Dried fish, fresh fish, and meat are consumed when available. Dried oysters (*vɔhɔs*) and a shellfish (*yet*) are used as ingredients of stews.

In Dakar, Bathurst, and other urban centres many European foods are commonly incorporated in Wolof cooking—potatoes, cabbages, tomato purée, macaroni, bay leaves (laurier in French, *lauri* in Wolof), and garlic. One typical lunch seen consisted of meat, groundnut oil, tomatoes, potatoes, cabbage, onions, pumpkin, garlic, garden egg, bay leaves, and European pepper.

Drink

Those who were not strict Muslims formerly made use of several types of local drink: mead, made from honey mixed with water and fermented in the sun; millet beer—boiling water was added to millet flour, the liquid then filtered and fermented —and palm wine. Imported trade brandy was generally preferred to all these. Mead and millet beer are no longer made. The favourite drink of the Muslims in former days was sugar and water. Now mineral waters manufactured in Bathurst

---

[23] *Ditah* is an extremely rich source of vitamin C.
[24] From the tree *gui*.
[25] *Neou*, a rich source of vitamin B1.
[26] For identifications of trees see p. 28.

ECONOMY 39

find considerable sale in Gambian trade centres. Lemonade is produced in Dakar for local use. A home-made ginger beer is in demand in the major towns of Senegambia. Coca-cola has established itself in Dakar, but made little impression in Bathurst.

Kola-nuts

Considerable amounts of kola-nuts, imported from Sierra Leone, are consumed by the Wolof. Kola has a rather bitter taste and, in quantity at any rate, has a slightly stimulating effect, alleviating the sensation of hunger and obviating thirst. It is, however, for its ritual and social significance that it is taken rather than for any physical effects. The consumption of kola increased with the spread of Islam and the Gambia Annual Report for 1863 mentions that the " Mohammedan . . . is firmly attached to the belief that should he die with a portion of the cola-nut in his stomach, his eternal happiness is secure." Kola-nuts are used on all important social occasions. They are given to a distinguished stranger. They are presented to a father when asking for his daughter in marriage. They are distributed as " alms " at funerals. A young man takes them to his girl friend (and her mother) when he goes visiting. They are brought to an elder when he is asked to settle a dispute. In all circumstances acceptance of kola symbolizes mutual goodwill.

Tobacco

A little local tobacco (*tamaka*) is grown, but most of the tobacco used is imported. The elders smoke pipes, using leaf tobacco, the young men cigarettes, both Players (Clippers), and French and Portuguese cigarettes. Formerly pipes were made locally, the bowl of baked clay with a reed stem; nowadays imported clay pipes are bought. Long ago it was apparently the women who smoked rather than the men, using " pipes longue d' une aulne,"[27] the men preferring snuff. At the present time women rarely smoke, apart from a few of the younger women in urban centres who have taken to smoking cigarettes, but often use snuff.

CRAFTS

Blacksmiths: The tools used in agriculture, with the exception of matchets which are generally of European origin, are made by local blacksmiths. The smith usually works in a low shed (*mbar*), his forge consisting of a charcoal fire animated by a pair of goatskin bellows. His basic tools are an anvil, hammers, files, pincers and tongs.

Silversmiths and Goldsmiths : The work of gold and silversmiths has a high reputation, especially for filigree work. Appia-Dabit (1943) has described and illustrated some Senegal jewellery. Ndiaga Thiam (1949) gives an account of the system of apprenticeship, and Bodiel Thiam (1950 and 1954) describes in detail the tools and techniques used.

Pottery : Water jars, steaming pots, bowls for washing and for use in dyeing, etc., are made by the women of the smith caste. Pottery is hand made—no potter's wheel being used—sun dried, and then baked in a pile of straw, cow dung, and chips of wood.

Leatherwork : For local use, leatherworkers make sandals, sheaths for knives, and covers for charms. For sale to Europeans, wallets, handbags, and covers for bottles and tins are made in the urban centres. Formerly saddles and horses' harness were locally made.

Weaving among the Wolof is often carried out by people of slave descent or *gewel*, though in some areas freeborn weave for their personal use. A narrow horizontal treadle loom is used, making a thick cotton cloth about 20 cm. wide.

Cotton is picked by women, cleaned by rolling out the seeds with an iron bar on a narrow block of wood, carded with European-made cotton cards, and spun into thread with a spindle.

[27] De la Courbe. 1685. p. 43.

In weaving, a man's occupation, both local yarns and imported yarns (generally coloured) are often mixed.

Dyeing is carried out by women. Nowadays indigo is purchased from the shops rather than grown locally.

Basketwork: A variety of basketwork—wickerwork, chequerwork, coiled basketry—is made by the Wolof. Winnowing baskets (*tɛntɛŋ*), open work baskets for carrying groundnuts (*sɛndɛl*), baskets of palm leaves (*damba*) for food storage, etc.

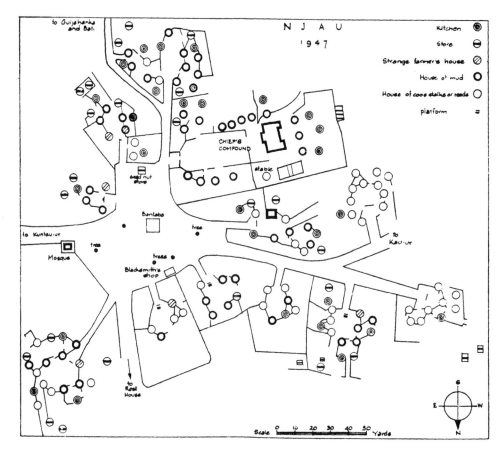

Woodwork: Mortars and pestles, wooden bowls and spoons, and canoes are generally made by the Laube, a gipsylike Fula-speaking people.

Hairdressing: Though all women know something of hairdressing, advanced hairdressing is in the hands of the smith or *gewɛl* women, who also manufacture wigs of fibre or wool. The woman having her hair done lies face downwards with her head between the knees of the hairdresser; the hair is undone with a metal spike, rubbed with butter or oil, and then reworked in the fashion desired.

Smiths, leatherworkers, potters, woodworkers are of low status in Wolof society.[28] On the other hand there is no social stigma attached to those who practice modern trades,[29]—European style carpenters, motor mechanics, electricians, etc.

[28] See p. 44.
[29] See Savonnet, 1955 (2), pp. 158-60, for a description of the position in a modern industrial enterprise.

SETTLEMENTS AND HOUSING

Rural Settlements

The characteristic layout of the Salum villages (see figure, p. 40) is as follows: the clusters of houses (*ker*, compounds, or yards) are grouped round an open village "square" which is shaded by baobab and cotton trees, but they are situated well back from it, and connected by fenced alleyways. The main road runs through the square. In the centre is the village *dat* or *pencha*, a roofed platform on which the men can rest in the heat of the day, where travellers pause for a rest and a chat, and where the young people of the village meet in the evening to play, sing, and dance. The *dat* is generally built under a shady tree, which is considered the residence of the village spirit. The women tend to gather at the well, and do not stop at the *pencha* unless they go there in the evening for singing or dancing. On the east is the mosque, surrounded by a high cane fence. Behind the mosque is the burial ground. On one side of the village square is often a blacksmith's forge, and sometimes near the village will be found a small hamlet occupied by Fulbe. Often the low caste groups—the smiths and leatherworkers—occupy a zone on the outskirts of the village.

The roads and paths into older villages are never quite straight, for evil spirits are believed to be able to move only in straight lines, and this helps to divert them, but new villages built by the members of the Mouride sect (see p. 70) are laid out with straight streets. Compared with Mandinka villages there is considerably more space between compounds—this lessens the risk from fire so common in Mandinka villages, and the whole layout is neater. Nor has a Wolof village the shapelessness of a Jola settlement in which the component hamlets may be scattered over distances ranging from a few hundred yards to a couple of miles.

The houses in the compound are generally grouped in a circle, the house of the compound head being opposite the entrance. Behind these houses are the kitchens and store rooms. When a man has several wives, each wife has her own house and kitchen. The houses of the strange farmers or those allocated to strangers are normally near the entrance. Across the passage way and a few feet back stands a screen of reeds or millet stalks, so that one cannot see directly into the compound. Besides ensuring privacy, this also has ritual significance, being designed to ward off spirits and prevent an evil eye from seeing in. Behind this fence there is often a small platform on which utensils, grain, etc., can be placed to dry. The fencing is made either of millet stalks or, occasionally, of reeds and is $5\frac{1}{2}$ to 6 ft. high, supported by wooden posts to which are fastened cross ties to hold the stalks vertical. Sometimes *krintiŋ* (woven bamboo) is used.

In Gambian Salum practically all the Wolof houses are circular,[30] though in the last few years there has been a tendency for the richer men to build rectangular houses. They are made either of mud, reeds, or millet stalks, and are about 12 to 16 ft. in diameter, with walls $5\frac{3}{4}$ ft. high. The roof is conical and about 6 ft. high, thatched with rhun palm leaves. The frame of the roof is constructed separately from the house, upside down, and, when tied together, is placed on the walls, the projection of the ends of the sticks holding it in place. Most houses have two doorways, the doors being made of cane, or millet stalks, more rarely of corrugated iron. The houses have no windows.

Married men's houses are generally of mud, those of the young men and women of cane, etc., though often old women occupy mud houses. Whitewash made from oyster shells is commonly used in the houses of richer people.

Unoccupied houses are sometimes used as stores, but normally an unroofed circular fenced enclosure is made, about the size of a house, with a low wooden platform 18 ins. high on which grain is stacked. This can be roofed over in the rainy season. Sometimes a large basket-like structure of interwoven branches is

---

[30] In the Senegal Wolof houses are now generally square, though in the writings of early authors, e.g., Baron Roger, 1828, they were described as round.

42 THE WOLOF OF SENEGAMBIA

made and raised off the ground. Large palm leaf baskets (*damba*) are also made for the storage of millet and rice, and may often be kept on a high platform. The clay storage jar (*buntungo*) found among the Mandinka and Serahuli is not used by the Wolof.

Furnishing in the houses is relatively simple. The beds consist of a framework of millet stalks, women bamboo (*krintiŋ*), or sticks of raffia palm, supported on forked sticks sunk into the ground. On this is laid either a mattress of sacking stuffed with straw or a mat. A few of the richer men have iron bedsteads. Mosquito nets of a light white cloth (*sanke*) are in general use, and most of the younger men also have sheets and pillows. Blankets are used in cold weather. Beside the bed there is often an old log of wood from the edge of a well, believed to bring good luck.

Most possessions—clothing, etc., are kept in locked wooden boxes raised off the ground on stones to prevent damage by white ants. The articles generally visible in a man's house are a hammock or a chair, a sheep or goatskin prayer mat, a kettle for ablutions before prayers, a water jar (generally raised on a forked stick or an old mortar) a fan or cow-tail to drive off flies and mosquitoes, and a kerosene lamp made from an old cigarette tin. A pole may be suspended from the roof, on which clothes are hung to dry, etc. Blades of tools are generally stuck in the thatch, or put on top of the house wall; seeds of various kinds are tied to the rafters, together with a host of charms, medicines, and objects of ritual importance, as well as articles of purely sentimental value, which are hung above the doors, over the bed, or placed between the rafters and the thatch.

In the kitchens and backyards are to be found the cooking places, consisting of three large stones, and the domestic utensils—iron pots, sieves, tin basins (these three generally being of European manufacture), wooden bowls, calabashes, clay pots with perforated bottoms used in steaming food, stirring sticks (swizzle sticks), ladles, winnowing baskets, figure 8-shaped calabashes, mortars and pestles, large tin basins for clothes washing, well ropes and well buckets (sometimes of tin, sometimes made from old inner tubes), bottles and tin cans, round blocks of wood used as stools, or low seats of raffia palm, boards on which groundnuts are ground into paste, a bottle serving as a rolling pin, water jars and drinking tins, covers of wood or coiled straw, brushes made from bundles of old millet heads or thin canes, low wooden blocks and clubs for beating clothes in lieu of ironing, though nowadays most people use flat irons heated on charcoal braziers.

In the kitchen there is generally a platform 5 to 6 ft. high over the cooking place on which utensils are kept. Goats are often tied to the posts of this platform at night. Wolof kitchens, though swept out from time to time, are by no means clean, and there is nothing like the standard of cleanliness of the Fulbe.

Urban Houses

In the towns and trading centres, as well as among chiefs and rich men in rural areas, the houses are of a different nature. The house of a moderately well-to-do Wolof is usually raised a foot or two off the ground, with one or two steps leading up. There is a wide veranda most of the way round, two main rooms, the inner being the bedroom of the house owner and a storage place, the outer a sitting room, though containing the beds of junior members of the household, which are used as couches in the daytime. The roof is of corrugated sheeting, the walls whitewashed, the floor cemented and covered with mats or linoleum. The windows may have expanded metal, and there is often a half door as in an Irish country house. Part of the veranda is enclosed and used as a lodging place for strangers. The kitchen is a separate building

The furniture consists of iron beds with mattresses, mosquito nets, sheets and pillows, the pillows often having texts and mottoes in excellent needlework. The walls are covered with pictures and photographs—prints illustrating Islamic stories; photographs of members of the household, of other Wolof (copies of photographs

ECONOMY

being made and sold in Dakar and other large urban centres), of local politicians (French and Gambian); pictures of members of the Royal Family and Winston Churchill (though not in Senegal); together with pages taken from illustrated magazines. European type chairs—upright chairs, armchairs often with cushions, or a deckchair, and a cupboard or sideboard on which is displayed a collection of crockery, a typical one having a teapot, coffee pot, thermos flask, jug and glasses, tin trays, basins, and an alarm clock. On the wall are fastened a clothes rack and a large mirror. Curtains are hung on the windows and doors.

In the larger towns, where numbers of strangers are lodged, a common form of subsidiary building is composed of a series of small rooms side by side with doors opening on to a veranda.

SOCIAL ORGANIZATION AND POLITICAL SYSTEM

SOCIAL ORGANIZATION

The main elements of Wolof social organization are their conception of descent, which may be traced either patrilineally or matrilineally; a hierarchical system of social classes, the major social strata being, with minor exceptions, endogamous; and a high degree of mobility, Wolof men often changing their place of residence. Age grouping is of limited importance.

SOCIAL STRATIFICATION

A broad outline of the old system of stratification is presented below, but does not pretend to incorporate all the minor shades of social differentiation. In some regions, for instance, there were various grades of nobles, depending on the nature of the rights they held, whether elective, territorial, or military. Under modern urban conditions the system has broken down, but in rural areas much of it still remains.

Freeborn (Jambur or gör)

  (i) Royal lineages, known as *garmi* in Walo, Kayor, and Baol, as *gelowar* in Sine-Salum, from which the rulers of the major Wolof states were chosen.
  (ii) Nobles, often related to a ruling lineage, or with the right to participate in the selection of a ruler, but not eligible themselves. Known as *dɔm i bur*[1] in Baol.
  (iii) Peasants, *badolo*.

Low-caste Groups (ɲɛnyo)

  (i) Smiths, *tega*. (*a*) Goldsmiths; (*b*) silversmiths; (*c*) blacksmiths.
  (ii) Leatherworkers, *ude*.
  (iii) Praisers, musicians, etc., *gewɛl*.

The low-caste groups of the Futa Toro Fulbe, the *Laube* (sing. *Labbo*), woodworkers; *aulube* (sing. *gaulo*), the praisers; and *wambabe* (sing. *bambado*), musicians; and the professional weavers, *mabo*, were also included in the Wolof scheme.

Even if a man did not practise the traditional craft of his father he did not lose his low status.

Slaves (jam)

In former days these were divided into two groups:—
  (i) Those born in the household.
  (ii) Those bought or captured in war.

Slaves also ranked according to the position of their masters, those of a ruler ranking highest, and those of the *gewɛl* and smiths, etc., lowest. Intermarriage apparently did not take place between the household slaves of a chief and those of the *ɲɛnyo*.

The position of royal lineages, which provided the rulers of the major Wolof states, is described in the account of the political organization. (See pp. 55–8.)

Nobility is considered a quality of birth, every noble being regarded as the descendant of a chief, but the quality diminishes, the more distant the relationship. Nobility formerly conferred certain rights such as participation in the election of rulers, the right to certain titles, and various military and territorial commands. In some cases the Wolof nobility had absorbed chiefs conquered by them, and intermarriage was common between the ruling families of the Wolof and Futa Toro Fulbe.

---

[1] *Dɔm i bur* signified " member of the royal lineage " in Jolof; " nobility " in Kayor; " the offspring of a noble father and common mother " in Sine-Salum.

SOCIAL ORGANIZATION AND POLITICAL SYSTEM 45

The *badolo* were freeborn, but possessed no power. At the present time the term has come to mean a poor or down-and-out person.

The smiths were men of considerable importance, for in the days of tribal warfare it was they who made bullets and lances and repaired guns. At naming and marriage ceremonies, etc., they are given presents and have the right to help themselves first when alms are being distributed. They act as intermediaries in settling disputes. The smith women are the potters. Owing to their comparatively small number, smiths have the reputation for contracting marriages within the legally prohibited degrees of kinship, though I have been unable to confirm this.

The *gewɛl* (or griots in Gambian English) include all musicians—no one other than a *gewɛl* would play a traditional musical instrument, though in small communities without resident *gewɛl*, smiths or men of slave origin may become drummers. Others specialize in shouting praises and reciting genealogies. Each major freeborn lineage has its attached *gewɛl* who know and recount its history. In former days the *gewɛl* accompanied chiefs to war and urged on their armies with martial songs (see example on p. 74). At public functions they sing the praises of chiefs and leading men, recounting their lineage, and the prowess of their ancestors in war, and entertain them and their visitors with music and song. Some specialize in story-telling, play-acting, or acrobatic dancing; others are buffoons whose work is to amuse the chiefs. A *gewɛl* in former days was often the confidant of a chief over whom he might exert strong influence by his powers of flattery. The *gewɛl* women are often hairdressers, and as such have the opportunity for learning and passing on all the local gossip. In the old days *gewɛl* had the right to mock anybody and could use insulting language without any action being taken against them. If a reward for their praises was not forthcoming or was considered insufficient, they were liable to switch to outspoken abuse, in consequence of which they were greatly feared and normally amassed considerable wealth. In modern times, and especially in urban conditions, this has changed, and open insults are not tolerated.

In the past they had a reputation for drunkenness and licentiousness and were long resistant to Islam. At death their bodies were not buried in the ground or thrown into the sea, for it was believed that in such cases the crops would fail or the fish die. Instead their bodies were deposited in hollow baobab trees. Now they are buried in a section of the cemetery apart from the rest of the community.

The slaves were formerly divided into two main categories, those captured in war and raids or bought, who could be treated in the worst possible fashion, and sold again if desired; and those born in the household, who were considered as inferior members of the family, their life being much the same as junior members of the household. The men cut wood and did most of the farming; the boys tended flocks, the women pounded grain, spun cotton, and fetched water. Weaving and many other crafts, e.g., basketry, were in their hands. The unmarried men (*surga*) and slaves often ate and worked together. A household slave could not be sold unless he had committed a crime, the punishment for which was banishment, i.e., murder, treason, witchcraft, etc. A slave worked for his master until marriage, the master providing a wife or marriage money, and gradually obtained a greater degree of independence as he became older.

The slave trade was suppressed with the establishment of the British and French Protectorates and slavery was officially abolished. The low social status of people of slave origin still remains, however, Islamic custom helping to maintain it (the period of mourning is shorter in the case of a person of slave origin, etc.), though no significant disability is now suffered by them. They no longer have to work for their masters and there is no restriction on their movements. The majority are proud of their status and keep up the client-protector relationship, helping their " masters " when extra labour is required, e.g., for thatching houses, etc., and playing their traditional roles on ceremonial occasions. In contrast to former days many hamlets now have *jam* as their *bɔrɔm deka* (village head).

46 THE WOLOF OF SENEGAMBIA

Intermarriage between free and slave does not normally take place, Islamic tradition holding that a woman should not marry below the status of her father. A chief or rich man can take a slave or *gewel* concubine (*tara*), who is then treated as a freeborn wife, but a freeborn woman would not normally marry a man of slave origin. Should she do so, not knowing that he was and found out subsequently, the marriage could be dissolved, the marriage-payment not being refundable. Should she marry him knowing his status, the marriage could not be dissolved on these grounds.

The old men of slave status acted as advisers to chiefs, published their orders and instructions, and saw that their commands were carried out. (See p. 57.) Slaves of the royal household enjoyed a greater degree of power than many a freeborn man, and could amass considerable property by demanding tribute in the name of their masters.

DESCENT GROUPS

The word for a relative, *mbɔka*, and the verb *bɔka*, to be related, carry no indication as to whether the maternal or paternal side or line is being referred to, unless some such phrase as *u ndei,* " mother's " or *u bai,* " father's " is added.

Certain terms are used for relationships between persons and to indicate kin groups, but are often used loosely in everyday speech.

Santa : patronymic. Family name transmitted through males. Used as a verb, *naka nga santa?* " How are you named? " Yoro Dyao uses it for "la famille par la filiation paternelle."

Gir : kinship traced on the father's side. The term does not seem' to be commonly used in Gambian Wolof, and was confused with *ger,* or *gör,* a word used in contrast to *gewel* and signifying "upper class, noble."

Genyo[2] : literally " belt." This is the commonest term in use for a group of patrilineal kin.

Askan : normally means homonym. Is used to indicate a group of people with the same family name, even though genealogical ties cannot actually be traced.

Men : literally " breast milk." Is used for a group traced matrilineally from a given female ancestor.

Het : kinship traced on the mother's side. Also used for nationality, species, etc.

A person's mother's brother's children are of his *het,*[3] but not his *men,* his father's sister's children of his *gir,*[4] but not his *genyo.*

Succession to ruling positions in the Wolof states was formerly transmitted largely through females. In Sine-Salum it was necessary for a claimant to be of *gelowar* origin through his mother, and no account was taken of the status of the father. In the three states of Baol, Kayor, and Walo the candidate for chieftainship had to belong to one of the noble matrilineages, and at the same time be descended in the male line from the first independent ruler[5] of the state.[6] Jolof was the one exception, in that succession followed the male line.

According to Sabatié (1926, p. 297) " dans le Oualo, où la succession échoit dans la ligne maternelle, les chefs et les principaux habitants se classent par Khet, et au lieu de dire habituellement nous sommes des N'Diaye, des M'Bodj, noms de familles paternelles, ils se dénomment des Tédiek, des Logres, des Djios, des Guigne, des Guignelar, des Sib, des Baor. Cette parenté et ces noms se communiquent par les femmes sans toutefois faire abandonner à leur porteurs le droit d'usage du

---

[2] Not to be confused with *ɲenyo,* low-caste group.

[3,4] *Het* and *gir* are clearly complementary terms, for one finds an old Wolof expression " *chi suma gir u bai ak suma het u ndei masula am ku def njekar lu ni mel.*" " By the *gir* of my father and the *het* of my mother there has never been anyone before who has committed such an abominable act."

[5] See p. 56.

[6] This situation sometimes led to a marriage between a man and his father's sister.

patronymique paternel s'appelant, lorsqu' on leur demande leur Sant, M'Bodj, N'Diaye ou Fal."

According to a Wolof saying, "it is the breast milk that determines relationship", and two children who are known to have sucked the same breast, even for a moment, are prohibited from marriage.

In some contexts the lineage of the father prevailed over that of the mother. The offspring of a slave mother and noble father were known as *dɔm i tara*, and formed a nobility of low status. A person of this class might come to occupy a position of authority, though he could be dispossessed by a brother whose mother was freeborn. An early example of this is quoted by Jobson.[7]

At the present time, with the Islamization of the Wolof, more attention is paid to patrilineal descent, which affects matters of inheritance and succession, but a man's *mɛn* still play an important part in his life. If he is in trouble, it is from his *mɛn* rather than his *gɛnyo* that he seeks assistance. If he develops leprosy or tuberculosis, it is to his mother's brother or his mother's kin that he will turn.

Some of the elements in Wolof kinship organization can be illustrated by examples from Gambian Salum.

(1) The first example from Buntung shows the effect of descent from a common ancestress in a compound of slave origin.

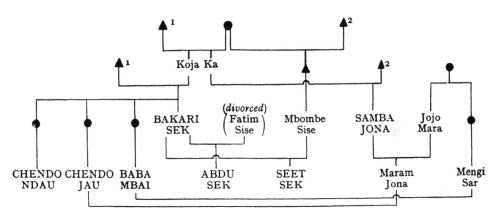

Adult males are shown in capital letters; adult females in lower case.
Numerals indicate first and second husbands.
Deceased persons: ● female   ▲ male.
|_____| marriage link.
(   ) now away.

Of the men now living together in this compound, Bakari was born at Gonkoro, Chendo Jau at Makagui, Baba Mbai at Porli, Samba Jona at Mbolgo, while Chendo Ndau came from Guijahanka. Men with five different patronymics, Sek, Jona, Jau, Mbai, and Ndau are to be found in the group. Its unity therefore depends neither on common birthplace nor patrilineal descent, but on their relationship with a common ancestress. In former days ownership of slaves followed the principle that whoever owned a woman owned her children, and in the days of slavery all the men named above would have been the slaves of one person. At the present time a client/patron relationship continues to exist between them and the lineage of their former "masters", who live in a neighbouring village.

[7] 1620, p. 80.

(2) A compound at Njau of settlers of slave origin showing the importance of ties to and through the mother.

In this compound, the head of which is Samba Sise, ties to and through the mother play an important part in its organization. Aliu So, is a son of Koja Ka by a former marriage, and though unrelated to Samba, remains in the compound with his mother. Samba's son, Omar, whose mother has been divorced, has not stayed with his father, but gone off to work on his own. On the death of Seni's first wife their small daughter, Loli, left the compound (though her paternal grandmother was there) and went to her maternal grandmother. The child of Demba Sise, who is married in a neighbouring village, spends most of his time here, and is looked after by his maternal

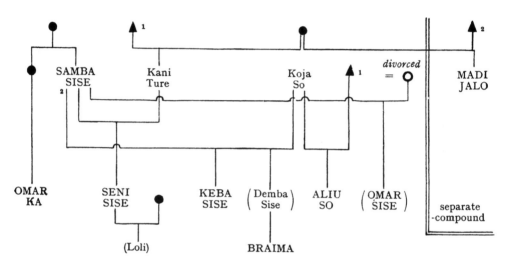

Males are shown in capital letters; females in lower case.
Numerals indicate first and second husbands.
Deceased persons ● female ▲ male.
|_____| marriage link.
(   ) now away.
For the sake of simplicity the wives and small children of ALIU, KEBA, and SENI have been omitted.

grandmother. Omar Ka, a young man, Samba's sister's son, has recently come to stay in the yard. When Seni had a quarrel with his father, when he wished to marry a wife of whom his father did not approve, he went to join his maternal uncle, Madi Jalo, who lived nearby, his mother also accompanying him. In spite of his father he married the girl concerned. They remained away for about a year after which a reconciliation took place.

(3) A co-residential group of warrior origin showing stress on patrilineal descent in succession to the chieftainship.

Among the freeborn, greater emphasis is placed on patrilineal ties. The lineage of the chiefs of Gambian Upper Salum shows how during the present century the chieftainship (passing from Sawalo to Omar Sira, to Laien, back to Omar, and then to Matar), and positions of authority, the Sergeant (i.e. the chief's executive and head of the Badge Messengers—the Native Authority Police), the Imam, etc., have been kept in a narrow segment of kinsfolk.

Mamud, Musa, and Seet (the Imam) occupy their own compounds close to Matar's. Mamud, the oldest man of the founding lineage, is the *bɔrɔm deka* (owner of

SOCIAL ORGANIZATION AND POLITICAL SYSTEM

the village) [8] but because he is blind the direction of village affairs is in the hands of an *alkali* (village head). Being in the village of a chief his powers are much more limited than they would be if he were in charge of a more remote village.

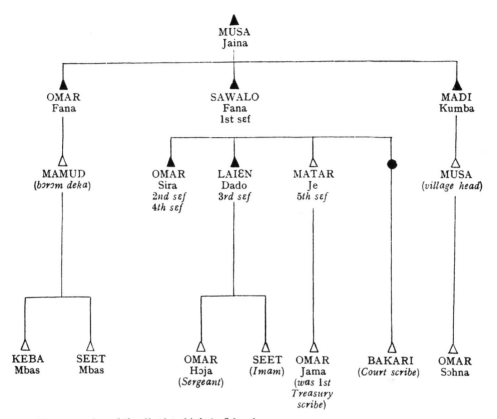

The succession of the district chiefs (*sεf*) has been:
1. Sawalo Fana .. .. .. resigned 1919, died 1924.
2. Omar Sira .. .. .. 1919–27.
3. Laiεn Dado .. .. .. 1927–28.
4. Omar Sira .. .. .. 1931–35.
5. Matar Je .. .. .. 1935 onwards;

with a period from 1928–31 when an outsider was appointed.

All the men in the above table have the same family name, Sise. Individuals with the same name and family name are distinguished by adding their mother's name to their own, the Omar Sises being known as Omar Fana, Omar Sira, Omar Hɔja, etc., Fana, Sira, and Hɔja being women's names.

Within the patrilineage there tends to be bitter competition between the children of different mothers [9] and secondly between the children of brothers for positions of authority. The consequence is that though the core of the lineage remains at Njau numerous segments have split off and migrated, not merely to other villages within the district, but to other districts. The descendants of Omar Fana, for example, by the four of his wives who had sons, are now each in a different village.

At the same time one finds individuals using the ties through their mothers to associate themselves with a powerful person or group.

[8] See p. 52.
[9] For an early example of this see p. 17.

In contrast to the modern situation, where succession to chieftainship generally follows the male line, emphasis was in former times placed on the female line. Taking an example from the history of Kayor we find the sequence shown in the following diagram.[10]

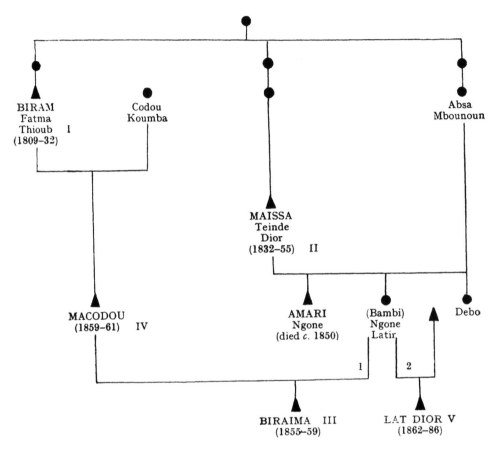

Male names in capitals; female names in lower case.
Numerals indicate first and second husbands.
I, II, etc., indicate succession.

Biram Fatma Thioub was followed as chief of Kayor by his " sister's " son, Maissa Teinde Dior, who prevented Macodou from succeeding his father. In order to secure the succession for his own son, Maissa married Biram's " sister " Absa, who was also his mother's " sister." Macodou married Ngone Latir, nicknamed Bambi, Absa's daughter. Maissa's son Amari Ngone died before his father, and Ngone Latir's son Biraima, deriving his rights as Absa's daughter's son and as Biram Fatma's grandson, followed. Macodou took over from his son, but ruled only two years, the chieftainship passing to another son of Ngone by a different husband. The example indicates certain of the characteristic features of succession in ruling lineages, the rivalry between son and sister's son, and marriages with close relatives across generations to secure the succession for one's own children.

[10] Based on Rousseau (1933) and Faidherbe (1883). The French spellings of names have been retained.

SOCIAL ORGANIZATION AND POLITICAL SYSTEM   51

Terms of Kinship and Affinity

mamat		great grandparent
mam		grandparent
bai		father (for father's brother see below)
ndei		mother (for mother's sister see below)
yai		mother (a more familiar term = mummy)
bajɛn		father's sister
nijai		mother's brother
raka		younger sibling or parallel cousin (see below)
mag, mak ..		elder sibling or parallel cousin (see below)
dɔm		child. The father and all his brothers call *dɔm* all the children born to any of them. The mother and all her sisters call *dɔm* all the children born to them.
set		grandchild
setat		great-grandchild
jerbat ..		brother's child (sister speaking) ; sister's child (brother speaking)
chamɛny ..		brother (sister speaking)
taau		first-born child
chaat		last-born child
yumpany ..		mother's brother's wife
jɛkɛr		husband
jabar		wife
wuja		co-wife
gɔrɔ		-in-law (father-in-law, mother-in-law, son-in-law, daughter-in-law, etc.)
pechergo ..		wife of husband's brother (an uncommon term)
jitle		step- ; e.g., *dɔm u jitle* stepson ; *ndei u jitle* stepmother

Where it is necessary to distinguish the sex the words *ju jigɛn*, female, *ju gor*, male, are added.

To indicate elder and younger brothers of one's father or husband, or elder and younger sisters of one's mother or wife, the words *ju mag* (*mak*)—elder or big, or *ju ndau*—small, are added to the appropriate term—e.g., *bai ju mag*, father's elder brother ; *jɛkɛr ju mag*, husband's elder brother.

The terms *raka* and *mag* have as their primary meaning, younger and elder. Used with a personal pronoun *suma mag, sa raka* " my elder ", " your younger ", etc., they indicate in the first place a sibling ; but they are also used of collateral kin on both the maternal and paternal sides. When a specific indication is necessary, it has to be described in some such terms as " his father and my father were of one father ", " her mother and my mother had one father, one mother ", and so on.

Ndei, bai, and *mam* are used in addressing people of generations older than oneself, e.g., *suma ndei*, my mother, and with their names in referring to them *bai Matar*, father Matar ; *ndei Kumba*, mother Kumba, whether they are actual kin or not. *Ndei* may also be used in preference to *mam* for old women. A mother's co-wives, and father's wives, are also addressed as *ndei*. *Tanta* (from the French " tante ") is commonly used as a respectful term of address to an older woman. The children of a household are normally spoken of as *halɛl yi*, or *hale yi*, " the children ".

Local Groups

The Village (*deka*)

The village consists of a series of compounds (*ker*) the layout of which is described on page 41. In Salum the settlements are small, generally consisting of one main patrilineage of freeborn with the descendants of slaves, a few members of the *ŋɛnyo*, and some immigrant settlers, though in some cases one finds a village predominantly

52   THE WOLOF OF SENEGAMBIA

of freeborn surrounded by a number of hamlets of slave origin. The ward organization typical of Mandinka villages is not characteristic, though occasionally found in some of the older and larger settlements.

The village head is known as the *bɔrɔm deka*, the owner of the village, and can either be the founder, the eldest living male descendant of the founder or, if these have emigrated or died out, the senior man in the village. Normally the *bɔrɔm deka* is also the administrative head, responsible for tax collection, and the general maintenance of law and order. If he is very old or blind, another member of his lineage acts for him, though it is usual to keep him informed and ask his advice (even if it is not followed) on important matters affecting the community.

During the native wars of the last century, settlements were larger than at the present day and generally stockaded, sometimes possessing a stone fort (*tata*) for the local chieftain. With the establishment of the French and British protectorates smaller settlements had nothing to fear from raids, and the creation of new villages has tended to increase.

Wives normally come to live in their husband's village,[11] but ties with their home villages are maintained by constant visits, especially during the dry season when they often go back to see their parents, or whenever a ceremony (a naming, marriage, etc.) provides the excuse for a visit.

Village Groups

In Pre-Protectorate days a number of villages were often grouped under the general supervision of a local chief (*sah-sah*) responsible to the *bur* (chief) for the collection of taxation. This system no longer obtains in present-day political organization, though for convenience a chief may sometimes station one of his henchmen in a remote area of his district to look after it.

The modern organization of Districts (in the Gambia) and of Subdivisions (in Senegal) has only a rough correspondence with former indigenous regional groupings.

MOBILITY

Apart from general migrations (see page 14), the Wolof show a high degree of mobility even within a small area, frequently changing their place of residence for one reason or another. Data provided by 33 men at Njau in Upper Salum showed the number of villages in which each had lived to be as follows :

No. of villages	1	2	3	4	5	6	7	12	
Cases	1	3	9	9	3	3	4	1	= 33

with an average of 4.

There was no apparent difference in mobility between the freeborn and those of slave descent, though the smiths and *gewɛl* appeared to have a greater tendency to change their place of residence.

The mobility of the Wolof is variously linked to economic, political, and other social factors. When pressure on land becomes noticeable, people tend to move to an area where agricultural opportunities are better. If a section of the people is at variance with a chief, many individuals may move off to another district. The desertion of a chief by his people is considered a great blow to his prestige, and in instances where the chief has exceeded his recognized powers, the threat to move is generally sufficient to bring him to reason. A run of bad luck may be attributed to supernatural factors, and a change made to get away from it ; or (rare nowadays) a man suspected of causing bad luck, i.e., of being a witch, may consider it advisable to move, until people's feelings have cooled.

---

[11] Exceptions occur when a man goes to live with his mother's brother and marries his daughter. Should he leave, the wife will, however, accompany him. Sometimes in modern urban conditions, presumably because of housing difficulties, one finds a man living in his wife's parents' compound.

SOCIAL ORGANIZATION AND POLITICAL SYSTEM

Those who are traders move seasonally to take advantage of economic opportunities. In the Gambia, traders who live in Bathurst during the rainy season go up river from November to March for the groundnut trade. Some then go to the Kombo region from March to June to purchase palm kernels. Many Wolof women from Bathurst go to the rice-growing areas from December to May to barter dried fish, peppers, tinned tomato purée, onions, kola nuts, etc., for rice. Similar movements take place in the Senegal.

AGE GROUPING

Though respect for elders is one of the ideals continually stressed, young men are free to work their own farms, go off as strange farmers, or set up as petty traders. They acquire independence at an earlier age than Mandinka or Jola.

The *kafo* (age-set system), so strongly organized in Mandinka society is not found in Wolof villages. Instead, for purposes of communal work an association (*kɔmpin*, from the English " company ") is called into action. This is an informal organization, having neither election nor initiation to membership, which includes most adult men aged from about 17 to 35, and cutting across the system of social stratification.

MARRIAGE

Polygyny is permitted by Muslim law. Chiefs tend to have the maximum number of legal wives together with as many concubines as they can afford, a relic of the pre-Islamic state of affairs. These are considered necessary both for purposes of prestige, and to perform the domestic duties required in a chief's compound where there are many dependants to be fed and visitors to be entertained. Village heads are also generally polygynous.

Among the Wolof in general, however, a high proportion have only one wife. Mandinka women hold that where there are two wives domestic duties can be shared and life is easier ; Wolof women rather take the attitude that where there is only one wife the husband will have more money to spend on her. Their attitudes and views are by no means consistent, for polygyny is acknowledged to lighten domestic work and enhance the prestige of their husbands.

For samples of men in a group of Upper Salum villages and Dakar [12] the extent of polygyny was as follows :

	One Wife			Two Wives			Three and Four Wives	
	58	..	..	14	..	..	2	
Upper Salum ..	..	78%	..	..	19%	..	..	3%
	593	..	..	181	..	..	46	
Dakar ..	..	..	72%	..	..	22%	..	.. 6%

The number of wives recorded in other samples is :—

Place	..	..	..	..	.. Thiès	..	.. Njau and Ballangar (Salum)
Author	..	..	..	..	.. Massé	..	.. Ames
Size of Sample	..	..	..	..	389	..	.. 84
Number of wives ..	0	..	..	23%	..	..	5%
	1	..	..	47	..	..	50
	2	..	..	21	..	..	25
	3	..	..	7	..	..	10
	4	..	..	1·5	..	..	7
	5	..	..	0·5	..	..	3
				100	..	..	100

---

[12] Massé, 1954.

THE WOLOF OF SENEGAMBIA

In the Thiès (an urban) sample there was great variation with socio-professional status. Farmers tended to be much married men, 10% bachelors, 90% married; while domestic servants and labourers had 54% bachelors and only 46% married. Presumably many labourers come to urban centres to earn money for marriage expenses.

In rural areas men marry fairly young, in their early twenties; in urban conditions, because of the higher cost of living, housing problems, and different value systems, marriage is often later. Youths complain of the difficulties of getting a wife while elderly men have two or three, but there are, after all, young women who prefer to be the second or third wife of a rich old man rather than do all the household work of a penniless young one.

In a polygynous household the first wife is known as the *awo*. She normally has the key to the granaries, divides out the grain daily among her co-wives, and superintends the work of the compound. The husband should not marry a second wife without consulting her, and she would be entitled to leave him should he do so. She assumes charge of the household should her husband be ill or away. Data from Njau showed that most second wives are widows (50%) or divorcées (33%).

Cross-cousin marriage is considered important among the freeborn families, less so among those of slave origin. A small sample from Njau in Upper Salum provides the following data:

		Closely related	Distantly related	Not related
Freeborn	..	6	1	—
Ŋɛnyo ..	..	1	—	2
Slave origin	..	2	—	16
		9	1	18

Marriage with a mother's brother's daughter took place in five of the nine instances, with a father's sister's daughter in four. Marriage with a relative is considered to produce a more stable relationship; disputes can be settled by kinsfolk and care must be taken not to offend a spouse who is also related.

The husband is responsible for the general maintenance of his wife and children, and the wife's personal property cannot be used by him for this purpose. If he has several wives, his attentions should be divided equally, if he gives a present to one, he should give a similar one to the other. The wives take it in turn to sleep with him and do the cooking.

The wife should fulfil the usual domestic duties, be faithful to her husband, carry out his instructions, and ask and follow his advice on important matters. The husband has the right to beat his wife should she deserve it.

JOKING RELATIONSHIPS [13]

There exists among the Wolof, along with other neighbouring peoples, a pattern of " joking relationships ".[14] In this particular area the relationship operates at different levels: across tribal boundaries, e.g., between Serer and Jola; between local groups, e.g., the people of Jarra and those of Nyomi; between patriclans, e.g., Njai and Job, etc.; and between cross-cousins.[15] Those in a joking relationship have the liberty to say anything they wish and to use what would normally be abusive language without any offence being taken at it. This type of behaviour usually operates only at festivals or ceremonies.

[13] See Labouret, 1941, pp. 140–4.
[14] *sanauya* in Mandinka.
[15] Ames, unpublished field notes.

SOCIAL ORGANIZATION AND POLITICAL SYSTEM

Among the Wolof the relationship is expressed in terms of *jam* (slave) and *bɔrɔm* (master), a father's sister's child will be *jam*, a mother's brother's child *bɔrɔm*. In clan relationships, the Njai are the *bɔrɔm* of the Gei, the Gei *bɔrɔm* of the Sɛka, the Sɛka *bɔrɔm* of the Job, and so on. On ceremonial occasions the *jam* come to help their *bɔrɔm*, and are rewarded for their services. At circumcision *jam* stay with their *bɔrɔm* during the period of seclusion, and are given clothing. When a woman is married her *jam*[16] perform dances for her, carry her loads to her husband's compound, and accompany her on ceremonial visits.

If a person happens to perform certain actions in the presence of one with whom he has a joking relationship, he commits *chalit*, and the *bɔrɔm* or *jam* has the right to take some of his property or demand a gift. Serious penalties can be imposed ; if a chief were to commit *chalit* a cow might be demanded. Such actions are : failing to call a person to join in eating ; leaving something behind after eating ; cutting a finger when using a knife.

FRIENDSHIP

Among the Wolof there are institutionalized friendships between members of the same sex, but especially between men. Such friendships are often formed in the circumcision shed or at school. The two friends tell each other their secrets, things they would not even tell their parents, exchange garments [17]—a sign of high favour— and help each other in times of trouble. A true friend should be prepared to give his aid even if it means breaking the law. It is not expected that one should have many friends of this nature.[18]

POLITICAL SYSTEM

The Wolof developed an elaborate system of government in which a " noble " class dominated the country, and elected rulers whose functions were to ensure the power of the state by leadership in war and to bring prosperity through the exercise of magical powers.

The religious wars of the last century between Muslims and pagans brought about the downfall of the old Wolof system, and this process was completed with the establishment of the British and French systems of government, but even at the present day one sometimes finds important survivals,[19] and attitudes and actions reminiscent of old times are occasionally to be observed.

CHIEFTAINSHIP AND GOVERNMENT IN THE WOLOF STATES

The earliest descriptions available of the Wolof chiefs occur in the writings of Cada Mosto (1455) :—[20]

" The kingdom [of Senega] is not hereditary, but commonly three or four lords (of which there are many in the country) chuse a king to their own liking, (yet always of noble parentage) who reigns as long as he pleases them. They often dethrone their kings by force, and the kings many times render themselves so powerful, as to stand on their defence. . . . This king has no certain revenues, but the lords of the country, to court his favour, make him presents every year of horses . . . and other beasts, such

---

[16] Real *jam* (descendants of household slaves) also take part in such ceremonies.

[17] Witches, sorcerers, etc., could work evil with sweat-stained garments.

[18] The Wolof philosopher Kɔche stated : " One sometimes has *one* friend, one never has several ", and gave as an example the tale of Mafal who, it seemed, had innumerable friends. To test them he went one night and knocked at the door of each, saying : " I am in great trouble. I have just killed the king's son." All drove him away in horror except one, who said, " Let us flee together ". I will help you to safety ", and was prepared to leave the bride he had just married and set out immediately (quoted by Bérenger-Féraud).

[19] Ames, for instance, has drawn attention to the fact that in Kahone the present chief of the canton is a descendant of the *Bur Salum* and that there are several old men living there who still hold traditional offices. (Personal communication, 1951.)

[20] Astley, 1745, vol. I, p. 581.

56 THE WOLOF OF SENEGAMBIA

as cows and goats ; also pulse, millet, and such like things. This king likewise lives by robberies, and forcing some of his subjects and those of neighbouring provinces into slavery ; part whereof he employs in cultivating the lands assigned him, and sells the rest to the Azanaghi and Arabian merchants, who trade here with horses, and other things, as well as to the Christians, since Trade has been opened between them.

" Every man here may entertain as many women as he pleases. The king has always upwards of thirty, and distinguishes them according to their descent, and the rank of the lords whose daughters they are. He keeps them in certain villages and places of his own, eight or ten together. Each of them has a separate house to dwell in, and a fixed number of young women to attend on her, with slaves to cultivate the land assigned her, that they may maintain themselves with the product thereof. They have likewise cows and goats, which the slaves also take care of ; and thus they sow, reap, and live.

" When the King comes to any of these villages, he brings no provisions along with him ; these women being obliged to bear the expences of him, and his retinue whenever he visits them. . . . Thus he travels from one place to another, visiting his women, by which means he has a very numerous issue. . . . "

A Wolof chief was treated with extreme respect by his subjects. When any person wished to speak with him, he had to approach slowly on his knees, the upper part of his body uncovered, and casting dust upon his head. Remaining bowed down he spoke in the most humble and respectful terms, still continuing to cover his face. The ruler would barely condescend to listen, and answered in only a few brief words. Even nobles were obliged to uncover their shoulders as a sign of respect. When a ruler appeared in public, he was always accompanied by a large number of courtiers and armed men.

The rulers of the Wolof states were chosen as follows :—In Jolof the *bur* had to be of the *genyo* (patrilineage) of " N'Dyadyane N'Dyaye ", the first ruler of Jolof. In Walo, Kayor, and Baol, the candidate had to be descended in the male line from the first ruler of the state [Barka Bo (Mboj) in Walo ; Amari Ngone Sobel Faal in Baol ; Dithié Fou N'Diogou [21] in Kayor], and in the female line had to be of *garmi* (see p. 44) origin. In these states the ruler was elected by the leading men of the noble families and could be deposed by them.

In Kayor, according to Boilat,[22] succession went from a chief to his brothers, then to the next generation. In Walo, from a chief to the eldest son of his sisters, though rivalry between sons and sisters' sons often resulted in armed conflict. In Walo a woman could succeed, taking the title of *bur*, while her husband was known as the " *marosso.*"

In Walo, Kayor, and Baol the ruler was elected by the leading men of the noble families and could be deposed by them. Sabatié [23] gives as the electors in Kayor a council of seven, three representing the freeborn, two the religious teachers (marabouts), one the warriors, and one the royal slaves. The characteristics looked for in a ruler were that he should be wise, clairvoyant (*ya bɔpa*), well liked, fairly rich, and of the appropriate descent.

In Sine and Salum, the *bur* had to be of *gelowar* (noble) origin through his mother, and was chosen by high ranking court officials, those of slave origin having an important say in his election. [24]

After being chosen, a Wolof ruler had to undergo certain rituals, designed to mark his change in status and to ensure the prosperity of his chiefdom. The new ruler was covered with amulets, drank magical powders, was purified by a bath,

---

[21] Détié Fou N'Diogou Faal in Diop; Dithie Fou N'Diogou in Rousseau. Dityé-Fou-Ndyogou in Gaden.

[22] 1853, p. 290.

[23] *c.* 1926, p. 312.

[24] Bourgeau, 1933.

SOCIAL ORGANIZATION AND POLITICAL SYSTEM

changed his garments for new ones,[25] was crowned with a special hat, and isolated for eight days.[26] Shoberl [27] described the accession of the *Damɛl* of Kayor as follows : " A very high heap of sand being thrown up, the prince, after being stripped almost naked, ascends with a run to the top of it, while his assembled subjects throw at him fruit, cotton, millet and other productions of the country, wishing that he may enjoy abundance of them during his reign." Robin [28] writing of Walo states " After his ' coronation,' if one might call it such, an official handed to the new *Brak* the royal insignia and these were, according to Yoro Diaw, a shield, a bow, spears and arrows . . . and a head of millet and seeds of various cultivated plants. . . . These insignia symbolized his powers and duties. He should be . . . brave in war . . . he should bring happiness and prosperity on his subjects."

Various ritual prohibitions were observed. Two powerful rulers were not supposed to see one another face to face. The *Brak* of Walo should not see the sea ; the *Damɛl* should not see a place called Gudes, and so on. A Wolof ruler had to be fit in body and mind. If he became blind he would be expected to resign, or could be deposed. On the other hand, in the later stages of the Wolof dynasties, drunkenness was characteristic of many of the rulers.

An account of the government of Walo is given by Robin.[29] The country was ruled by the *Brak* assisted by the " *seb-ak-bawar*," which consisted of the representatives of three noble matriclans. The major officials were the *jaudin*,[30] the successor to the rights of the indigenous rulers (the *laman*), in charge of the land ; the *jɔgomai*,[30] in charge of river affairs, taxes on fishing, etc. ; and the *malo*, the treasurer. These had the power to elect or depose the *Brak*. He could be deposed if the country was ravaged by wars, famines, civil discord, etc. De La Courbe (1685) describes the position of the *malo* saying " Malo was the greatest noble of the country, who establishes and dethrones the king when it pleases him and is like the controller of his actions," and mentions as other officials Guiodin (=*jaúdin*) and Membrose, apparently the chief of a certain region. The *Brak* assumed leadership of the people in war, but only appeared in public at the festival of Mohammed's birthday. The country was also divided into chiefdoms ruled by *kangam* (vassal chiefs) nominated by the *Brak* with the approval of the *seb-ak-bawar*.

Labouret [31] has given a description of the positions and functions of the officials of the *Burba Jɔlɔf*.

In Salum the major officials of the *bur* were :—*Jaraf ju rei* (" Grand Diaraf ", " Jagaraf ", etc.), who was freeborn but not of royal blood. He was an elector of the *bur* and acted as his advisor. He represented the freeborn people of the chiefdom and was their protector. He was also a judge with power to impose the death penalty. Should the occasion arise he could depose the *bur*.

Farba ju rei ; of slave status, and nominated by the *bur;* directed military expeditions.

Farba bir ker (sometimes known as *jolige*) ; looked after the palace (*pei*) and its finances ; of slave origin, and chosen by the *bur ;* carried out sentences imposed by the *bur* or *Jaraf ju rei* ; in charge of the jail.

Jaraf bekanɛg (" *beukeneck* "),[32] " Chamberlain" ; could be either freeborn or slave. He was in charge of the servants ; attended to their food and dress, received visitors. He looked after the household in the *bur*'s absence.

Each of the major low-caste groups, the smiths, leatherworkers, griots, Laube (Fulbe woodworkers) had their leading men (*farba ude, farba tega*, etc.) with whom

[25] Labouret, 1941, p. 87.
[26] See Bérenger-Féraud, 1879, p. 46, for ceremonies in Kayor; p. 52 for ceremonies in Walo.
[27] Vol. II, p. 61 (early 19th century).
[28] 1946, p. 255.
[29] 1946.
[30] " Diawdin " and " Diogomay " in Robin.
[31] 1941, pp. 87–89.
[32] Corresponds to *Biset* (mentioned by Labouret) in Jolof.

58 THE WOLOF OF SENEGAMBIA

the *bur* dealt when he had any matter concerning their group. Relations with the Fulbe were carried out through the intermediacy of a *jolige* (" dialigue ").

Local chiefs in charge of groups of villages were known as *sah-sah*. These were appointed by the *bur*, but were not of noble origin. Leading warriors were known as *saltige*.

Those in charge of trade centres were called *alkati*. In former days this word was used almost in the sense of ambassador or intermediary between Europeans and Wolof chiefs.[33]

The *bur* gave guns, horses, and wives to his local chiefs and leading warriors. In return they collected taxes—cattle, grain, native cloth—keeping a share for themselves, directed communal work, etc., and entertained the *bur* and his entourage on his travels.

The income of the *bur* was derived from taxes on traders, cattle from the Fulbe (whom he protected against raids by other chiefs) ; fines from the punishment of crimes, including profits on people sold into slavery as a punishment ; presents from those who wished to win his favour ; tribute from peoples recently conquered ; gifts from neighbouring states which wished to remain on good terms ; general requisitions of grain, livestock, etc. ; the property of strangers who died in his territory, and in the case of coastal rulers, property cast on shore from the sea (including human beings).

Wolof rulers, both *burs*, and lesser chiefs, had to show themselves strong and rich. Otherwise they ran the risk of being displaced. They therefore surrounded themselves with warriors,[34] dependants, and *gewɛl*, who both constituted their power and were a sign of it. The dependants of the chiefs, the young unmarried men, were known as *surga*, while the warriors, often of slave origin, were called *dak* (*dag*).

The head of the women in the chiefdom had the title of *linger* (" Lynguere, Linguere "). She was normally the *bur*'s mother, or in some cases a sister. In Jolof she could be a father's sister, or cousin on the paternal side. She had a number of dependent villages which cultivated her farms and paid tribute to her, her personal entourage, and her own court concerned with women's matters, e.g., cases of adultery. The chief wife of the *bur* was known as the *awo*.[35]

The *bur* could also choose a potential successor, *bumi*, who thereby acquired a certain amount of power. Often he was in charge of raids and of levying taxation. The electors, however, were not bound to select him.

The *bur* was buried in secret in his house or compound, the burial place being known only to close relatives. His successor was elected by the *jaraf ju rei* in consultation with the major court officials. The news of the death of the *bur* was published five days later by drum, to avoid possible invasions from neighbouring states during an interregnum. The corpse was simulated and carried to the burial ground, after which feasting, drinking, and dancing took place.

Law

Civil Disputes

In civil disputes, most of which are matrimonial cases—divorces, or refunds of marriage money—efforts are first made to settle the case without recourse to formal courts.

---

[33] Barbot, writing of Rufisco in the 17th century, states: " Several of the king Damel's officers generally reside here, and have a chief over them, call'd Alcaide by the Portuguese and natives, the name importing a governor to administer justice, who is assisted by a Gerafo, as his deputy. These two jointly manage the government, collect the king's customs, toll, anchorage and other duties. . . ." Labat describes the Alquie . . . " c'est ainsi qu'on appelle les Capitaines des troupes nègres; qui outre cette charge avait encore celle de Secretaire d'État pour les affaires étrangères, c'est à dire pour celles que le Roy a avec les Blancs qui trafiquent dans ses États."

[34] In former days the soldiery—known as " *Tiedos* " (*Chedo*)—formed a drunken and licentious, anti-Islamic element in the population.

[35] See p. 54.

SOCIAL ORGANIZATION AND POLITICAL SYSTEM

If there is a dispute between a husband and wife, kinsfolk will try to settle it. The head of the lineage may be consulted, if available, or sometimes a father, elder brother or maternal uncle, or there may be a gathering of various kinsfolk. The initiative may be taken by the wife, the husband, or any senior relative. An elder will state what customary procedure demands, propose a commonsense solution, and may bring about a reconciliation, if not immediately, at least after some further talk to conciliate both parties. If no solution is likely to be reached, a more formal meeting of elders may be called, or the matter may be taken to court. Here again, the first efforts of the court members are generally to try to achieve a compromise. The matter may be argued out publicly, but end apparently without a decision, the court leaving it to the elders of the families concerned to work out a solution satisfactory to both parties. If this cannot be achieved the matter may be returned to court for a formal decision.[36]

Criminal Procedure

In former days the death penalty could be imposed by the *jaraf ju rei* for treason witchcraft, and homicide. For theft, following Islamic law, the hands could be amputated but generally criminals were banished, i.e., sold into slavery.

Trial by ordeal was practised, a red hot iron being applied to the arm after it had been rubbed with palm oil. If the person was injured he was declared guilty, if uninjured, innocent.

In the Gambia, with the establishment of the Protectorate, native courts were instituted under the presidency of the District Chief and with leading men of the district as Court Members. A copy of the court judgements are sent monthly to the Commissioner (Administrative Officer) and they can be revised by him either on his own initiative or on the application of the parties concerned. If it is considered necessary, he can order the case to be retried, or have it transferred to a Protectorate Court. Sentences of imprisonment of more than 14 days have to be confirmed by the Commissioner.

A detailed description of the organization, competence, and functions of the native courts in Senegal is to be found in Chabas, " La justice indigène en Afrique Occidentale Française."

Marriage Law

Prohibited degrees of marriage. In accordance with Islamic law, marriage is prohibited between relatives in a direct line, between brother and sister, uncle and niece, aunt and nephew. A man cannot marry two sisters (unless one has died), his father's widow, his son's widow, or the daughter of one of his wives by another man. By Wolof custom two children who have sucked the same breast are debarred from marriage.

Invalid marriages. A marriage will be annulled if (a) it is not consummated ; (b) if a previous marriage of the woman is still valid, i.e., if she marries a second husband without a legal divorce from her first ; (c) if a spouse before the marriage is consummated is found to be suffering from madness, leprosy, or elephantiasis ; (d) if an incestuous marriage has taken place.

A man is prohibited from marrying a widow or divorcée during the *idda* period (i.e., the period of seclusion prescribed by Islamic law) and should he do so the marriage will not be valid.

Repudiation and divorce. The husband can repudiate his wife by saying the appropriate formula of Islamic law in the presence of witnesses, or by using some such expression as " I regard you as my mother." A woman has to ask for a divorce in the chief's court. The repudiated wife can take away her personal property, and if pregnant is entitled to support during pregnancy, as well as to a contribution to the maintenance of the child.

[36] Following Chabas, 1952, pp. 474–7; his description fits the Gambian position.

THE WOLOF OF SENEGAMBIA

A divorce can be demanded by the woman on the following grounds :—

(a) Failure of the husband to complete the marriage-payment within the agreed time.

(b) Impotence of the husband. To solve this delicate question tribunals often make the husband and wife spend a night together in a special room and report on the result. The husband may be given a period varying from a few months to a year in which to seek a cure. If a cure is not achieved, a divorce will be granted.

(c) Where a marriage has been contracted between a Muslim and non-Muslim, and the non-Muslim has subsequently not become converted.

(d) Where the husband has represented himself to be freeborn, but has turned out to be of low-caste status. (This cannot be used as grounds for divorce when a woman marries knowing her husband to be of lower status than herself.)

(e) When the husband has become mad, affected by leprosy, elephantiasis, etc.

(f) Long absence of the husband without support. Should the wife marry again, and the husband reappear, she may be given the choice of joining him again.

(g) Lack of maintenance—failure to provide adequate food and clothing.

(h) Ill-treatment, undue discrimination in favour of her co-wives ; serious abuse (e.g., where the husband has unjustifiably accused her of adultery or witch-craft) ; excessive beatings (when a wife has failed in her duties a reasonable beating would be considered justified).

The marriage money is not repayable if the fault lies with the husband. If the wife wishes for a divorce purely on the grounds that she dislikes her husband, she will have to refund the marriage money.

When a wife feels she is being badly treated she usually goes back to her parents and stays there. After a while, the husband sends to ask either for the return of his wife, or his money, and discussions are opened between the families concerned as to whether she was justified in leaving, whether she should return, and if so, on what conditions, until either an amicable settlement is reached or divorce decided on.

Adultery. In the case of adultery by the wife the man can divorce her and claim repayment of the marriage money ; content himself with damages, or take the matter to court where adultery is treated as a criminal offence. The wife and her lover can be beaten if caught in a compromising situation. The damages payable by the lover will depend on a number of circumstances : the social status of the parties, whether the husband had been neglectful, on the amount of encouragement given by the woman, the place where the adultery took place, and so on.

Custody of children. After divorce children remain with the mother, boys until they are seven, girls until they are 15 or 16. The father remains responsible for giving his daughters in marriage, even if they are living apart from him with their mother.

INHERITANCE [37]

Under strict Muslim law an heir must be a legitimate relative of the deceased, and an illegitimate child cannot inherit. As far as one can see, however, illegitimate children are treated by native custom in the same way as others. An unborn child is entitled to inherit, and when the estate is shared out the proportion of a male child is set aside. If the child turns out to be a daughter the amount given to her is reduced.

It would seem that the heirs normally pay the debts of the deceased provided a prompt claim is made. Any marriage money owed by the deceased is payable before other debts, and the creditors are paid in the order in which they present themselves.

---

[37] A detailed account of the laws of inheritance among the Wolof has now been given by Chabas. See *Annales Africaines*, No. 1, 1956, pp. 75–119.

SOCIAL ORGANIZATION AND POLITICAL SYSTEM 61

The remainder is then shared out following Malekite law, a learned man being called on to assist, and being rewarded with a present for his help.

Sometimes customary law prevails. If a man dies his brother may take over the whole of his compound and property, marry his brother's widows, and assume responsibility for his children. Marriage with a brother's widow is, nevertheless, not as frequent among the Wolof as among the Mandinka.

LIFE CYCLE [1]

BIRTH

A woman gives birth in a squatting position, generally on the bare floor or on a piece of sacking. In the case of a first pregnancy birth may take place in her mother's compound. Lasnet says that the women walk up and down and pound grain in a mortar to provoke the final labour pains. Men are not permitted to be present. The midwife (*forkat*) cuts the umbilical cord with a metal knife. The afterbirth and sacking are buried in the back yard. The baby is then washed. The umbilical cord, especially in the case of a first child, may be made into a charm which is worn by the child. Before returning to sit on the bed, the mother performs the rite of jumping over the fire, which she does in four directions. The midwife then holds out the child to the mother three times, but does not give it to her until the fourth time. This is believed to prevent madness. Before the child sucks it is given a charm (*nasi*) to drink, consisting of a verse from the Koran which has been written on a wooden slate and washed off with water. A goat is killed for the mother on the day she gives birth.

During the first week numerous ritual precautions are taken. A fire burns continuously night and day in the house. An iron rod (*jɛlɛm*), used in pressing the seeds out of cotton, is stuck into the ground beside the fire, though some do this only if the mother is still suffering pain. A pot containing pieces of the plant *rat* is kept beside the fire. Water in which *rat* has been boiled is drunk for abdominal pains. Branches of *rat* are put outside the door of the house, and of *dogut* or *wɛn* across the door of the house and the entrance to the compound. The knife used to cut the umbilical cord is kept under the baby's pillow, or if the knife is not available, any metal instrument. During the first week the mother and child remain indoors. Should necessity compel her to go out, she carries the knife with her and leaves a broom of stalks (*pɛt-pɛt*) near the baby's head.

NAMING CEREMONY

The naming of a child takes place a week after its birth ; if it was born on a Wednesday, it will be named on a Wednesday.

During the week messengers are sent, or the father goes himself, to inform friends and relatives in neighbouring villages. In the case of a first-born child a large gathering can be expected ; if several previous children have been born the ceremony is much less elaborate. A ceremony held in the dry season when there is little work has much more time given to it than one during the farming season. The ceremony takes place in the compound where the baby was born, normally about ten or eleven o'clock in the morning.

On the morning of the naming day, the fire which has been kept burning in the mother's house is extinguished and swept out by the mother. She bathes, and the child is washed with medicine, water in which various items—leaves, grass, bark, and a silver ring—have been put. The baby is sometimes washed first with soap and water. Visitors begin to arrive and make gifts of small coins and produce to the mother, if women ; or to the father, if men.

For the naming ceremony a mat is spread out in the centre of the compound, and an old woman, often the midwife, brings the child covered with a white cloth out of the hut, and sits down on the mat, legs extended, and holds the child in her lap. Next follows the shaving of the baby's head. Usually this is done by someone of low caste or slave status. The baby's head is wet with water ; the knife which has been used for cutting the umbilical cord is first touched to its head, then an ordinary knife is used for the shaving, which is begun on the right side. Beside the old woman is a clay bowl containing red and white kola nuts, cotton, and *suna* (early millet), red kola signifying long life, white kola good luck, while the *suna* and cotton are crops considered " blessed." The hair is carefully gathered up, lest witches should get hold

---

[1] Based mainly on material from Salum.

LIFE CYCLE

of it and work some evil against the child. The shaver is also rewarded with kola. Sometimes the child's head is shaved in private before strangers arrive.

When the shaving has been completed an elderly or learned man rubs his hands over the child's head, prays, and spits in its ears to implant the name in its head. On occasion several elderly men pray together over it. The name of the child is announced to the crowd, and prayers are said that it may have long life and prosperity. A " charity " (alms) of kola nuts, cakes of rice flour, etc., is given out, the oldest of the men of slave descent being in charge of the distribution.

In the case of a first child, where there is a big gathering to celebrate the event, the baby and its mother are hidden away from the crowd, lest someone with the evil eye should see them.

An animal, generally a sheep or a goat, is killed in honour of the occasion. In many Mandinka communities, this must be killed at the exact moment that the shaving of the baby's head is begun. In Wolof communities the animal is killed after the shaving. Food is distributed to the guests, and the rest of the day is spent feasting and dancing.

WOLOF NAMES

The Wolof have both first names (*tur*) and family names (*santa*) i.e., patronymic names.[2] On analysing these one finds many which are those of neighbouring peoples— Fulbe, Mandinka, Serer, etc. This may be due to the absorption of many slaves of foreign origin, the assimilation of strangers, or merely linguistic borrowing. One often cannot tell whether a given *santa* was originally Wolof, Serer, or Lebu.

Kobès gives as Wolof: *Bajan, Bahum, Chal, Cham, Chau, Jago, Jaham, Jase* (leatherworker), *Jɛng, Job, Jon, Juf, Fal, Fay, Gay, Gey, Gise, Mboj, Mbow* (leatherworker), *Ndau, Ndong, Ndur, Njai, Ngom* (*gewɛl*), *Nyang, Nying, Nyas* (smith), *Pui, Sala, Sar, Seka, Sen, Sila, Sise, Sou, Tole, Ture.*

Sabatié gives as the principal Wolof *santa* :—in Jolof: *Mbɛng, Ndiaye, Niang, Ndao, Tob ;* Ganar : *Ouad, Diop, Fal ;* Walo : *Mbodj, Diao, Gay ;* Kayor : *Fal, Gay, Nias, Sar, Seck ;* Baol: *Fal ;* Salum : *Mbodj, Diao, Ndao ;* Dakar : *Diop ;* Rufisque : *Mbaye.*

The *santa* of the original Lebu families in the Dakar peninsula according to Angrand [2A] are : *Badiane* (=*Bajan*) ; *Diagne, Diène, Dione* (=*Jon*), *Diop* (=*Job*), *Gueye* (=*Gey*), *Mbenga, Ndoye,* and *Paye.*

Serer names include *Sar, Chor, Juf, Fai, Ndur, Ngom,* and *Sen.*

Many *santa* have a " praise form " used in greetings and praises. This trait is also found among the Fulbe and Mandinka. The praise form for Job (Diop) is *Jamba Job,* for Njai, *Njai Gainde* (Njai lion). Sise and Ture both have the Mandinka form *Sise Manding Mori, Ture Mori* (Sise the learned men of Manding, Ture the scholars), though the Sises also use *Sise Ngari* (presumably from the Fula *ngari,* a bull).

The people of each patronymic group also have animals, etc., associated with them which they are prohibited from harming or touching, e.g., Njai—the lion ; Job—the crown bird ; Ture—the frog ; Ndur—the hyaena. Should they do so they believe trouble will be sure to fall on them.

As a large number of people have the same family name—about one in three in Upper Salum is a Sise—it is usual to refer to individuals by their first name followed by their mother's name, e.g., *Omar Sira, Omar Rɔhi,* instead of calling both *Omar Sise.* Sometimes a nickname is used.

Common Wolof first names are :—

For the men—*Abdulai (Abdu), Alasan (Asan),*[3] *Ali, Aliu, Amat, Babukar (Babu), Dauda, Dɛmba, Dudu, Ibu, Laiɛn, Madi, Malik, Mamat, Mamadu, Matar, Musa, Mustafa, Omar, Samba, Sawalo, Seni (Usenu),*[3] *Sidi, Suleman, Tijan, Usman.*

---

[2] The names of *hɛt* (matri-clans) do not seem to have been systematically studied. See. however, p. 46.

[2A] Angrand, 1946, pp. 24–25.

[3] Names given to twins.

64 THE WOLOF OF SENEGAMBIA

For the women: *Adam*,[3A] *Aida, Aisatu (Satu), Aminata (Ami), Binta, Fana, Fatim, Fatumata (Fatu), Hadi, Hauwa*,[3A] *Hencha, Hɔja, Hɔreja, Jainaba, Jama, Jara, Je, Jojo, Juli, Kumba, Kura, Lɔli, Mariama (Yama), Maram, Ndumbe, Ramatulai, Sɔhna, Suna, Yasin.*

The majority of these names are of Islamic origin.

Sometimes where a woman has had a succession of stillbirths or children dying at an early age, the next child may be given a name like *Sen* (rubbish heap), or *Buguma* (I don't want).

CARRYING A CHILD FOR THE FIRST TIME

A minor ceremony takes place when a child is carried on the back for the first time. Apart from the participants no one else takes much interest in it. The ceremony is held on the evening of the naming day. A small girl is called, preferably one whose brothers and sisters are living, the baby is held over her back but not touching it, while a *jɛlɛm* (iron rod), and a *pɛt-pɛt* (broom) are dropped four times between the baby and the girl to remove any possible evil influences. A liquid charm (*nasi*) is sprinkled on the child's back, and the baby is tied on with an ordinary cloth used for baby-carrying. The girl then goes from the compound into the street four times and picks up sticks or stalks of millet which are brought back to the house and burnt in the evening.

CIRCUMCISION [4]

Though female initiation takes place among the Mandinka and Jola, there is no such ceremony for Wolof women.

Boys are normally circumcised when aged between eight and twelve, though formerly in the southern zone, circumcision was often not performed until a young man was ready for marriage. Some of the Islamic teachers, on the other hand, have their children circumcised at a very early age, though later these generally take part in the circumcision ceremonies along with their age mates.

The features correspond with those of neighbouring Mandinka and Fulbe. The ceremonies take place during the dry season after the groundnut crop has been sold. Learned men choose an auspicious time. The boys visit relatives to inform them of the event, and there is special drumming and dancing each evening for a week beforehand.

Circumcision takes place in the bush, and no women are allowed near. The boys are washed with medicine, and taken out of the village early in the morning, clothed in white, often escorted by their *jam* (father's sister's sons). They are expected to show no sign of fear, and it is considered meritorious for a boy to run away to be circumcised without the knowledge of his relatives, though the operation would not be performed until they had been told of his action and given their consent. The circumcisor, *ŋaman*, is sometimes a Pullo [5] or a blacksmith. The sons of the highest ranking men are operated on first.

A shed (*mbar*) is built near the village, where the boys (now known as *njuli*) stay until their wounds are healed. Women are not permitted to approach the shed, with the exception of the girl who brings water when the boys are temporarily away. Numerous ritual precautions are taken. A man with second sight (*kumah*) stays with the *njuli* day and night to prevent interference by witches. Special charms are made. A fire is kept burning continuously. It is a great disaster should a *njuli* die in the *mbar*. He would be considered unclean and buried in the bush, not in the regular cemetery.

[3A] Names given to twins.
[4] Material on circumcision has been published by De la Courbe (1685), N'Doye (1948), A. G. Thiam (1952), and Jectson (1952). This account has been limited to what is generally known and what can be seen by women.
[5] Singular of Fulbe.

LIFE CYCLE

The dress of a *njuli* consists of a white robe and a triangular-shaped hat of native cloth. He should never be bareheaded. He carries a thin rod in one hand, has a small ladle-shaped calabash hung round his neck, two sticks which he carries tied to the wrist, and a circular cover (*paka*) which he holds in front of his face if he comes near a woman. When greeting an elder he has to crouch down and touch his forehead to the ground. A *njuli* remains unwashed to avert the attention of malevolent spirits.

The *njuli* are looked after by *sɛlbe* (older boys, often cross-cousins) and *kɔrɔŋ-kɔrɔŋ* (circumcised boys of their own age, who are their close companions, and perform many services for them). The youth in charge of the *sɛlbe*, the *botal*, superintends the division of food, regulates the comings and goings of the boys, and renews the wound dressings. The father who initiated the proceedings determines when the major ceremonies shall take place.

In the evenings the *njuli* are taught various songs and beaten by the *sɛlbe* should they fail to learn them properly. Several days after entering the *mbar* the boys take part in a ceremony called *dɛm tɛn*, in which they go to the well and dip their rods in water left out by the girls for that purpose. Thereafter they have the right to chase and beat the girls of the village.

The *sɛlbe* form a society (*kompin*, derived from the word " company "), the members holding such positions as Governor, Commissioner, Chief, Judge, Doctor, policemen, lawyers, customs officials, etc. Minor disputes are settled by the various authorities, and fines are inflicted for infringements of custom, e.g., failure to present a gift when visiting the *mbar* for the first time.

The first major ceremony in which the whole village is involved occurs with the appearance of a monster (*mam*) who comes to " eat " the boys. The monster is heard roaring in the night, and as it approaches the village, the women and girls rush indoors and hide. Later the *sɛlbe* visit the village, beat on the cane house walls with their sticks until the women of compounds with boys in the *mbar* produce some *kungutu* (cake), hurriedly shutting their doors once they have done so. During the night a tall pole, 20 feet high or so, with a pot on the top is set up outside the *mbar*. This is called the *sɔchu mam*, the chew-stick of *mam*.

The next major ceremony is the *Samba sɔho* which can be witnessed by women. The *sɛlbe* begin by performing a whipping dance. They parade rhythmically round the *sɔchu mam* with a long thin stick in each hand ; from time to time one stands still while another gives him a stroke on the back. The women come from the village, and the *njuli* are led out of the *mbar* and kneel down behind their *kɔrɔŋ-kɔrɔŋ*. The *njuli* then dance individually for a short spell to the accompaniment of the women's clapping, after which the women dance in return. At sunset they are chased back to the village, and the boys go back to their shed.

In the final ceremony, the shed is burnt early in the morning, and the boys are taken off to bathe. They put on new trousers and have their heads shaved into distinctive patterns. Henceforth they are known as *huhaha*. Later in the day they return to the village, and go in procession to the mosque, squatting down in front of it. *Suna* and cotton (the blessed crops) are put on their heads, and water sprinkled over them. The Imam thanks everybody for their help, and prayers are said. The boys then have the privilege of rushing off to seize any fowl on which they can lay their hands.

For several days they remain in their distinctive dress, going round greeting relatives and receiving presents, after which they resume normal life.

Marriage

Betrothal

The first marriage of a young man is generally arranged by his parents and he has little say in the matter, the eldest son, in the case of freeborn, normally marrying a cross-cousin. Sometimes a youth may go to his father and tell him he has met a

66 THE WOLOF OF SENEGAMBIA

girl whom he loves and wishes to marry. Fortune-tellers are consulted as to whether the pair are likely to be temperamentally suitable. Enquiries are made by an inter-mediary—a friend, a family slave, or a cross-cousin—who goes with a gift of kola nuts to find out whether the girl and her mother are favourable to the proposition and, if so, kola nuts are formally sent (*guru nuyu*) to the father with a request for his daughter in marriage. In theory (i.e., according to Islamic law) the father has the right to marry off his daughter even without her consent, provided she is still a virgin. In practice, this is not enforced.[6] On receiving the kola, he asks his daughter and her mother if they agree to the marriage and, unless they object, he gives his consent and shares the kola among the people of the compound, friends, and neigh-bours. The man may now begin courting the girl. Each time he visits the compound he should bring presents of kola, etc., and he must provide the girl with new dresses for the main festivals of the year, but if marriage negotiations are broken off, such presents are not returnable. He may also perform services for his father-in-law, providing help in weeding, house-building, thatching, etc. If he does not show himself generous during this period, the girl and her mother may begin encouraging other suitors.

Later, a further payment, *ndah i far*, to drive off rivals, is demanded by the mother and father. In accepting this they indicate that the suitor now has the sole right to court the girl.

Taka (Tying the marriage)

The Muslim religious ceremony is generally held on a Friday after the mosque service and is performed by the Imam in the bride's compound or in that of her patrilineage head. Her father or guardian, and the future husband's father or guardian, and witnesses must be present. The woman's presence is not required, and the groom is usually absent.

A formal request for the woman in marriage is made. This request is granted, and the amount of the marriage-payments is discussed. A payment of 99 kola nuts and 17s. is made by the groom's representatives, 1s. going to the Imam, and 16s. to the bride. Kolas are distributed to those present, and sent to absent kinsfolk. If the full marriage money is paid on the spot, the husband may take the bride back to his home or village almost immediately, but this does not usually happen unless she is a widow or divorcée. Usually there is a delay of several months between the " tying " of the marriage and the transfer of the bride to her husband's home.

Dancing, feasting, and firing of guns may follow in celebration.

The Marriage-Payments

The marriage-payments made by the husband consist firstly of what is called the " dowry " in Gambian English, which in Salum is generally £20 in the case of a freeborn woman, £16 in the case of people of slave origin, and £30 for chiefly families ; and secondly a host of minor payments. These include payment to the girl for orna-ments (£4) ; to her mother (£2) ; to her father (£2) ; perhaps to a paternal aunt (10s.) ; for kola nuts (£2 10s. or so) ; and gifts to members of the *ɲɛnyo*, together with mats for the bride's use during the ceremonies. If the girl is going to another village presents have also to be made to her age mates.[7] A lesser sum is payable in

---

[6] By French law (Decret of 15 juin 1939) the consent of the spouses is indispensable to the validity of a marriage.

[7] In Bathurst the total varies from £37 17s. to £50. The former sum includes the " dowry " (£20), " expenses " (£17), and the 16s. paid to the bride. Anderson in his *Islamic Law in Africa* (1954) writes: "It is not at all easy to decide what terms to employ for these different payments. It seems, however, that Muslims in the Gambia regard both the larger payment (of £20, etc.) and the smaller payment (of sixteen shillings) as constituting the Islamic dower (*sadaq* or *mahr*)—the latter representing the ' minimum ' dower of Maliki law, on the payment of which they insist at the time of the contract, and the former the balance

LIFE CYCLE

respect of a widow. Only £4 or £6 would be paid when a man marries his brother's widow. In the case of divorcées the position is variable. If a woman has broken off her marriage in order to marry another man, she will have to pay back the " dowry " plus expenses, and the new husband may have to pay an increased " dowry." Robin [8] quotes an example in the Senegal where, by this process, the total of the various sums paid out on one girl eventually passed a million francs CFA.

The " dowry " is divided between the bride's mother and father and is used to provide the articles that the girl takes with her to her husband's place, her household utensils and clothing.

Once the marriage has been tied, the husband may legitimately have intercourse with his wife, but she does not yet go to his compound, he has to visit her in her parent's home.

Mur (covering the bride) or *chet*

The transfer of the bride does not normally take place until the marriage-payments have been completed. However, should the husband's family be in urgent need of another woman in the house to carry out essential domestic duties, the bride's parents may consent to her joining her husband. This is known as *aba* (to borrow). She would, however, have to return to her parents for the final ceremony, the *mur*, which is the covering of the bride and her formal transfer to her husband's home. This normally takes place towards the end of the dry season, and on the night of Thursday/Friday. During the Thursday evening the bride remains indoors in her mother's house, while her *jam* (both of slave descent and father's sister's daughters) dance and sing for her. Later the old women of the compound bathe her and clothe her in white. Traditionally the bride weeps and shows great reluctance to leave her home. Next her head is covered with a white pagn (native cloth). She is then escorted by her mother and sisters to a mat spread out in the compound and made to sit down. The elders give her advice—to be faithful to her husband, to respect him and the men of his yard, to be obedient and carry out his commands, and to be as good as her mother was before her. Prayers are said that the marriage may be happy and fruitful. The bridal party, the girl escorted by her age mates, friends, *jam*, etc., and a few elderly women, moves slowly towards the groom's house, the men firing guns, the girls singing ribald songs. They should arrive there in the early hours of the morning. The party first of all goes round the *pencha* (the abode of the village spirit) four times, and then enters the groom's compound. Here the bride is formally handed over to the elders of her husband's yard, who are enjoined to treat her well, and regard her as a daughter.

Meanwhile the husband is waiting in his home to which the bride is taken. Various rites [9] are performed using salt, cool water, and grain, to ensure that the husband's family will develop a " taste " for the girl, that the marriage will be " cool," i.e., free from quarrels, and fruitful.

In the morning if the girl is a virgin, the husband puts a gift under her pillow. The elderly women who accompanied the bride come for the blood-stained sheet which they take back to the girl's mother who is congratulated on her daughter's good behaviour. In former days the sheet was exhibited in the village accompanied by singing and dancing, though this custom has now died out. Virginity may be demanded

---

of the dower customarily payable, which may be deferred. In pure Shari'a there is, of course, no need for minimum dower to be paid where a larger sum is also provided, but the Malikis regard it as reprehensible for a bride to permit consummation of marriage before she has received at least minimum dower. This may be the origin here; while it is also possible that the £20 represents an Islamicized form of the normal African ' bride-wealth '." In translations of the Koran (e.g., Mauli Muhammed Ali's translation of 1935), the word " dowry " is generally used.

[8] Robin, 1947, p. 197.

[9] Described in detail by Ames, 1956, p. 165.

68 THE WOLOF OF SENEGAMBIA

as a condition of the marriage, and if a girl has lapsed from virtue the husband can demand an immediate divorce.

During the following week further ceremonies take place, designed both to ensure fertility and prosperity and to symbolize the assumption of domestic duties. The bride remains indoors most of the time surrounded by her female companions and *jam*. If the husband is a rich man, a goat is killed each day.

On the day after the *mur*, a procession comes over from the bride's mother's home bringing her possessions, mortar, pestle, winnowing-basket, sifter, tin basins, iron pots, calabashes, ladles, mats, boxes of clothes, etc. Next the bride, still covered and accompanied by her companions etc., formally visits the various compounds of the village, paying her respects to the elderly women and yard heads. On the third day the *bulufɛli* [10] takes place. The bride puts on her best dresses, and wears her white bridal covering, but shows her face for the first time. During the *bulufɛli* ceremonies grain is poured symbolically over the bride's hands into a mortar to ensure fertility. Then a close female relative of the bride is handed prayer beads, a relative of the groom an axe head, which they throw into the mortar at a given signal. The first to fall is believed to indicate the sex of the bride's first child.

Finally the bride visits the well, dressed in her best clothes and wearing a head shawl, to pay her respects to the spirit of the well. She washes herself, and performs the symbolic washing of one of her pagns (skirts) and one of the groom's garments, after which one of her companions takes over and finishes the task. The bride returns to the village, where a feast is prepared.

When a woman has once performed the *mur* ceremonies they are not repeated for later marriages.

Other Forms of Marriage

Apart from normal marriage there are several noteworthy variations.

(*a*) Marriage by capture (*gef*). In former days when a man and woman were in love but her parents opposed the match, the man arranged to have her carried away by a party of horsemen, and subsequently sent a message to say what he had done. In time this seems to have turned into a simple runaway marriage. Runaway marriages are said to have been common in former days, but are now rare.

(*b*) Marriages to cement political alliances. Two chiefs, to establish a closer alliance, may each marry a daughter of the other.

(*c*) A daughter may also be given to a noted religious teacher as a sign of honour. In such a case the marriage ceremony is performed but no marriage money is paid apart from the sum of 16s. when the marriage is tied. As the daughter will occupy a privileged position—in the next world as well as in this—she is unlikely to object to such a marriage.

DEATH

Funeral ceremonies are similar to those of other Muslim peoples of the Senegambian region. When a person has died the women of the compound raise the death cry, which summons people to his yard. The elders pray and make arrangements for the burial, send messengers to inform kinsfolk and friends in neighbouring villages, and dispatch young men to dig the grave. If a person dies late at night, someone remains in the house with the body and a fire and lamp are kept burning.

When the time for burial draws near, the corpse is taken to the back yard to be ritually washed by a person of the same sex as the deceased, with water drawn fresh from the well. The orifices are closed with cotton. A few drops of perfume are sprinkled on the body and it is clothed in a white shroud, generally of locally made cloth.

The body is then rolled in a mat, carried on men's shoulders, and taken to the mosque, where it is laid on the ground outside the mosque facing east on its right

[10] Described in detail by Ames, 1956, p. 166–7.

LIFE CYCLE 69

side. Women do not accompany the funeral procession though a few elderly women may attend at a distance during the mosque service. The dead man's name is announced, and the Imam asks the people to say what they know about him. Relatives and friends state that they knew him to be a good Muslim and praise him. The elders line up in front of the mosque and pray, though the young men present remain seated.

When the prayer is finished all rise and the corpse is carried to the burial ground. All those present squat and bow down as the body is slowly lowered into the grave, where two men stand to receive it. The mat is unrolled from the body which is laid on its right side facing east. Leaves and sticks are put across the grave, some sticks being stuck into the side walls to take the weight. Earth is heaped on top. Water is brought for those concerned to wash their hands. After the body has been lowered into the grave further prayers are said, after which those present, as a final gesture, throw a small stone or piece of earth over which they have said a prayer, on to the grave. The mourners do not look back, for angels are believed to visit the grave as soon as they have turned their backs. They return to the mosque where a charity of kola nuts and cakes is given out. Shares are given to the grave-diggers, then the smiths, followed by the elders and representatives from other villages. Charity is also given out on the 3rd and 8th days, and, if the deceased was an important man, on the 40th. The grave is protected from hyaenas by wooden posts and thorny branches. In former days the burial was apparently followed by drumming, dancing, and feasting, though this may have been a Serer custom rather than typical Wolof.

Formerly, *gewɛl* were buried in hollow baobab trees. Stillborn children are buried in the compound, people drowned in the river at the nearest suitable spot on the river bank. The bodies of those drowned or burnt to death are not washed.

The period of mourning is four months and ten days for freeborn women, two months and five days for women of slave origin. During this time the widow should remain indoors or in her compound as much as possible. She does not have her hair done in a fashionable style or wear ornaments. No mourning procedure is carried out by a man for a dead wife.

RELIGION

ISLAM

Monod states that the " Islamization of the Wolof chiefs which enabled them to shelter their subjects from the ' holy wars ' of the Mauretanians, should be placed between the end of the XIth century, the date at which Islam was planted firmly on the banks of the Senegal by the Almoravides, and the XVth century." The Wolof chieftains are described by the early Portuguese writers as having Muslim teachers (Mauretanians) as members of their entourage, though many chiefs considered that the rules of Islamic teaching did not apply to them personally. Le Maire (1682) writes that the nobles are more attached to the Muslim religion though " it is but little observed by the common people, who have only a smattering of it."

However, the early conversion was very superficial, and it was mainly the magical aspect of Islamic culture that took root. Saugnier writing in 1791 says : " Les nègres Yolofs du Sénégal sont ou Chrétiens ou Mahométans, ou plutôt l'un et l'autre, ou encore mieux ni l'un ni l'autre ; la religion leur est égale." Though Islam spread sporadically it was not until the religious wars of the latter half of the 19th century that widespread conversion was achieved. Subsequently the establishment of French and British rule enabled religious teachers to move freely, and spread Islam more widely.

Islam as practised in the Senegambian region has been described in detail in the works of P. Marty and A. Gouilly. Of the Islamic brotherhoods, both the Qadiriya and the more recent Tidjaniya have their adherents, but among the Wolof a relatively new sect—Mouridism [1]—has become one of the most active forces in Senegal. Founded in Baol by a Tukulor religious teacher Sɛriny Amadu Bamba about 1886–9, it is based on the total submission of the individual to his spiritual chief (*sɛriny*), who fulfils the necessary religious duties on his behalf, takes over the direction of his earthly life, and in return guarantees his salvation in the next. Instead of despising agriculture like many Muslim peoples, the *sɛriny* here make it one of the essential conditions of sanctification, and their followers are organized so as to obtain the maximum benefit from their labour to an extent unknown in pagan villages. The possibilities of mechanized agriculture have also seized the imagination of the Mouride leaders—for good or ill. The result is that they have become an extremely powerful economic force, their colonies, often of young men and women drawn away from their parent villages, spreading eastwards and southwards and opening up new land for cultivation. One of the largest mosques in negro Africa has been built at Touba (in Baol) and this has become the centre of an annual pilgrimage which attracts an increasing number of people each year. In 1956 it was estimated that 250,000 people congregated for the pilgrimage.[2]

Among the Gambian Wolof the main tenets of Islam are adhered to : the fast month is generally observed, though if it falls in the farming season the young men often break their fast. The five daily rites are performed regularly. The religious festivals (Tabaski, and the feast at the end of the Fast Month) are the occasions of great celebrations. Alms are given generously to the blind, the aged and helpless, lepers, and to twins. Some, however, do not observe the prohibition on alcohol, for small bottles of alcohol are always on sale in the trade centres and markets, and brandy is highly esteemed as medicine.

Boys from about seven onwards are given religious instruction, for which purpose they are sent to a teacher. They are taught the prayers, though they have often acquired these already through imitating their elders ; they learn passages of the Koran by heart ; and are instructed how to write Arabic characters, and copy portions of the Koran. For writing they use wooden boards, a reed pen, and an ink made from soot, which can be washed off. Their instruction takes place by firelight in the early

---

[1] See in particular P. Marty: *Les Mourides d'Amadou Bamba* (1913).
[2] *West Africa*, Oct. 27, 1956, p. 846.

RELIGION

71

morning and at night. Strict discipline is maintained by the master. In the day-time they collect firewood, and help on their teacher's farm.

PAGAN BELIEFS AND PRACTICES

R. G. V. [3] [de Villeneuve] (1814) describes as one of the greatest festivals of the year in Sine, the honours paid to the memory of former sovereigns. The *bur* went out on horseback, accompanied by his entourage and with drums beating and horns blowing, followed by the people. On the tomb of his ancestors he poured brandy and wine and scattered millet. In the evening guns were fired, and cavalry displays took place, followed by dancing at night.

In spite of the impact of Islam, there is still a much deeper layer of pagan belief and observance among the Wolof than among the Mandinka or Torobe. Wolof men and women are loaded with amulets, round the waist, neck, arms, legs, both for protection against all sorts of possible evils, and to help them to achieve certain desires. Most frequently these contain a paper on which a religious teacher has written a passage from the Koran, or a diagram from a book on Arabic mysticism, which is then enveloped in paper, glued down, and covered with leather, but some-times they enclose a piece of bone or wood, a powder, or an animal claw.[4]

It is not considered good to praise a child for the parents fear that some evil might happen to it—one should say that the child is ugly. After its naming a child may be hidden away from the crowd for fear of the evil eye. One should not call a person by name at night in case witches hear it, and work some evil on him. Divination of various kinds is common—interpretation of dreams [5]; throwing cowrie shells (often done by women, and of about the same standing as reading fortunes in tea leaves) ; consulting Islamic almanacs ; interpreting signs and omens—cocks crowing at unusual times, owls hooting, birds appearing at certain times,[6] etc.

Witches (*dema*) are greatly feared. Witchcraft is inherited matrilineally—a person whose mother is *dema* is *dema*. A person whose father is *dema*, but mother is not, is a *nɔhɔr*, and is reputed to have second sight, but is considered incapable of doing harm. Witches eat people's souls and drink their blood, causing them to waste away. They can take the form of owls and hyaenas (which dig up bodies from grave-yards), or even appear as " bad breezes." In former days suspected witches were tortured to make them confess. Nowadays this has ceased, but public opinion may still lead to a suspected witch leaving the district until tempers are cooler.

Belief in a wide variety of supernatural beings exists :—

(*a*) Spirits of ancestors, who can appear in dreams, and to whom libations are sometimes made.

(*b*) Spirits of villages or specific localities (*rab*), which may manifest themselves in visible form, e.g., as a large snake.

(*c*) The devil (*seitane*) who makes people mad, and who may steal a child and substitute a deformed or abnormal infant.

(*d*) Spirits (*jine*). There are a great variety of spirits—some good, some evil, some mischievous. Wolof stories tell of humans who were taken to the spirit world (e.g., the story of the midwife related by Equilbecq), or of people against whom their relatives have turned, being befriended by spirits and given riches before returning home. Sometimes a female spirit appears to a human in the form of a beautiful woman, a dangerous situation usually resulting in the man being driven mad.[7] Spirits may live in the earth or under the sea. They are believed to move especially at mid-

---

[3] Vol. 3, p. 133.

[4] Le Maire, writing of 1682, states that the " nobles, above all, have their shirts and caps covered with them, and they cover themselves with them to such a degree, that they are often obliged to be placed on horseback."

[5] See Holas, 1949.

[6] For examples see Appia, 1940.

[7] See Cendrars, 1947.

72 THE WOLOF OF SENEGAMBIA

night or midday, and to be about at twilight, when extra precautions are taken against them.

(e) *Kɔndɔrɔŋ.* The *kɔndɔrɔŋ* are dwarfs with long beards and feet back to front who look after and protect wild animals. If a human being comes across one, it might challenge him to a wrestling match, throwing him and leaving him unconscious.

(f) *Ninkinanka.* This is a fabulous snake of immense size dwelling in the depths of the forest or swamps. Anyone who sees him dies.

Belief in these beings is also found among the Mandinka, Fulbe, etc., while the devil and *jine* are shared with the Muslim world.

Angrand [8] mentions a cult of " *Ntambes,*" spirits intermediate between humans and a supreme God. Each family had a special " *Ntambe,*" sometimes several. Among the nobles, to the " *Ntambes* de famille paternelle s'ajoutaient ceux de la famille par filiation utérine." The " *Ntambes* " were believed to be capable of manifesting themselves. The cult was exercised by the " *Yahouminbini,*" priests and diviners possessed of a magical power derived from the spirits.

In some areas, while the men are Muslim, the women have retained an earlier cult of spirit possession. This is described by Balandier and Gorer. After the first signs of possession, dances of exorcism, " *ndeup,*" are performed under the supervision of the " mistress of the spirits," the dances being followed by a sacrifice.

A mixture of Islam and paganism is also characteristic of Salum. Before the farming season there is a religious ceremony, the men meet at the mosque, alms are given out, and prayers said for a successful farming season, a ceremony which is probably an adaptation of an old pagan one. If a drought occurs, the men go to the mosque to pray (the salat-al-istisqa) but if this does not have the desired effect, the women perform a rain dance, dressed up in rags, or in men's clothes, and wearing ornaments made from rubbish. They then go out of the village in procession, the children gather branches of trees or shrubs, and on their return beat the grave of the founder of the village with their branches.

CHRISTIANITY

A few Christian Wolof, mainly Roman Catholics, are to be found in the urban centres, Dakar,[9] Saint-Louis, Bathurst, etc. From the time of the earliest Portuguese contacts efforts have been made to convert the Wolof to Christianity, but with little success. " Cada Mosto told him . . . that the religion of Mohammed was false, and the Romish, the true one. This made the Arabs mad, and Budomel laugh, who, on this occasion, said, that he looked upon the religion of the Europeans to be good ; for that none but God could have given them so much riches and understanding. He added, however, that the Mohammedan law must be also good ; and that he believed the Negros were more sure of salvation than the Christians, because God was a just Lord ; and, therefore, as he had given the latter Paradise in this world, it ought to be possessed, in the world to come, by the Negros, who had scarce any thing here, in comparison of the others." [10] Such sentiments one may still hear even at the present day.

A number of the local preachers and laymen who played a prominent part in the establishment of the Methodist Mission in Bathurst during the last century were freed Wolof slaves.[11]

---

[8] He follows Yoro Dyao as quoted by Gaden, 1912, p. 137.
[9] Details of the early missionary activity in Senegal are given in Boilat: *Esquisses sénégalaises,* pp. 20–34.
[10] Astley, I, p. 585.
[11] Fox, p. 359.

OTHER CULTURAL FEATURES

DRESS AND APPEARANCE

Huxley [1] describes the dress of the Wolof women in Bathurst as follows : " Their long, satiny gowns glow boldly on mahogany skins ; gowns of cerise and apple green, gold and magenta, electric blue, iris purple and claret red, cut in the Empire style, with square necks and many flounces down the wide sleeves. Over their dresses most women wear white muslin slips, absolutely clean and creaseless, through which the colours glint and shine."

It is a sign of smartness to wear several dresses on top of one another, each a little shorter than the one below it, giving a voluminous appearance to the wearer.

On their heads the women wear brightly coloured head-ties (scarves) tied in a great variety of fashions. Unmarried girls normally go bareheaded.

The most striking feature of the women is their elaborate hair styles. Small girls may have their heads shaved into various patterns. In former times some of these patterns indicated the patronymic group to which a person belonged. Those with the family name Job (Diop) often had a single tuft of hair left above the forehead in imitation of the Crown bird—the Job " totem." Older girls have their hair plaited into various ringlets, or wear " horns " of false hair, to which are tied coins and beads. Adult women often wear wigs, made from sisal, from black four-ply wool (*lɛɛn*), or in the most recent fashion, of black velvet (*ulur*). Middle-aged women generally have large " buns " on either side of the head. Normally the forehead is shaved, and the head-tie is fastened high up on the forehead in contrast to the Mandinka style where it comes just above the eyebrows.

Eyebrows are blackened—in the latest style the brow is continued in a curve down to the cheekbone—and a blue line is marked under the lower eyelids by kohl or antimony, making the eyes appear larger. The lower lips of the women, and sometimes the gums are tattooed blue, which is highly effective against their black skins. Palms of hands, soles of the feet, and nails are stained with henna.

To the hair are tied gold ornaments, large gold ear-rings hang from their ears, while smaller rings are often fastened round the outside of the ear. Rings are worn on the fingers, and bracelets on the arms. On special occasions elaborate gold necklaces are put on. (Some of these ornaments are described and illustrated by Appia-Dabit (1943). Strings of beads are worn round the waist, preferably so many that they can be heard to make a noise when the wearer makes a sudden movement.

In urban centres the women dress well for their daily visits to the market, but special displays of finery are reserved for festivals, visiting times at hospitals (especially on a Sunday afternoon), and election activities (registering as voters, election meetings, voting, and celebrating the results). Even the poorest women keep a special dress for such occasions. In rural areas the women on everyday occasions wear a heavy skirt of locally woven material, and a dress of imported cloth.

Characteristic of the Wolof are the postures and gestures adopted by their women, features extremely difficult to describe, e.g., the transformation of spitting into an elegant and superbly performed, even if unhygienic, gesture ; their mode of walking with a slightly shuffling step ; the air of magnificent nonchalance with which they move through the streets.

The Wolof men wear much the same dress as other Muslims of the Gambia and Senegal, baggy trousers, and long robes, either a *haftan*, or an open sided *waramba*. The Wolof tend to use rather more cloth than the Mandinka, their garments being wider and looser. On the head, younger men wear woollen " Pullman caps " or felt hats, older men fezzes or hats of white cloth. Sophisticated young men wear sun-helmets. In rural areas the men when working on the farms wear an open sided shirt of locally woven cloth, and short baggy trousers of the same material. The

[1] 1954, p. 6.

74   THE WOLOF OF SENEGAMBIA

men either shave their heads or have their hair cut short. Small boys up to about five go naked, then a loincloth is worn, and a few years afterwards, shorts. Girls begin to wear a skirt when aged three or four. In the towns, however, small boys wear shirts and shorts at an early age, and naked children are now becoming rare. Sandals of various types are worn, some with soles of wooden blocks, others made from old motor tyres. Moroccan type sandals are worn by the richer and more elderly men. Many wear European canvas shoes. Chiefs on special occasions often wear locally made ornamented leather boots.

CHARACTER

While it is a rash undertaking to attempt to describe the " character " of a people, there are nevertheless certain traits—attitudes and reactions, interests expressed in conversation, ideals illustrated by tradition, moral values, etc.—which distinguish the Wolof from neighbouring peoples.

All travellers from earliest times mention the generosity and hospitality of the Wolof. Mollien (1820, p. 89) writes : " Hospitality is so generally practised . . . that it is not regarded by them as a virtue, but as a duty imposed on all mankind ; they exercise it with a generosity which has no bounds, and do not even make a merit of it."

In former days they had a great reputation for bravery and daring. Cada Mosto, quoted by Astley (p. 582), wrote : " They are extremely bold and fierce, choosing rather to be killed, than to save their lives by flight. They are not afraid to die, nor scared as other people are, when they see a companion slain." A griot (praise singer)'s song recorded by Reade (1864) extols the brave : " I go in front. I fear not death. I am not afraid. If I die, I will take my blood to bathe my head. The man who fears nothing marches always in front, and is never hit by the murderous ball. The coward hides himself behind a bush and is killed. Go to the battle. It is not lead that kills. It is Fate that strikes us, and which makes us die." At the same time, a career in Colonial forces with its constant discipline does not today appeal to the Wolof.

Gorer (p. 16) gives by far the most penetrating analysis of Wolof character in recent times : " The most marked moral characteristic of the Wolof is pride, or dignity ; even their appearance is redolent of it. This sense of personal dignity is almost universal from the richest to the poorest—there is as yet no feeling of class difference founded on wealth—and is universally respected by the Wolof . . . " This sense of pride is at times coupled with an over-sensitiveness which makes them see insults and intrigues where none were intended. Their intense pride has also meant that their long contact with Europeans has not resulted in a rapid disintegration of their own culture, and other African peoples coming into the Wolof sphere of influence, with the exception of the cattle-keeping Fulbe, have generally ended by adopting Wolof ways and, if a Wolof ancestor can be traced, by calling themselves Wolof.

Gorer writes (p. 17) that the Wolof are " much preoccupied with money ; it is one of the most constant words in their conversation. They do not value it for its own sake, however ; as soon as they have paid their taxes and their debts they will employ whatever money they possess in gifts and in ostentation. When the groundnut cultivators were making a great deal of money they would as soon as they were paid ransack the shops for the most expensive perfumes, clothes, cigars ; they would flaunt these till they had been seen by everyone and then discard them, and wait in comparative poverty till the next harvest. The idea of hoarding or saving is quite alien to them." Though not a universal characteristic of the Wolof, these characteristics are often to be observed.

Gorer further states (p. 18) that " the Wolof have a great admiration for cunning. Many of their anecdotes—and their conversation takes largely that form—are concerned with successful tricks. It is usually the story of how a cripple—particularly blind men, who are credited with great sharpness—a poor man or a weak man gets the better of his stronger and richer neighbours. No moral judgement is implied in

OTHER CULTURAL FEATURES

these tales of sharp practice but merely admiration for uncommon wit . . . " An example given by Mollien (p. 55) illustrates this : " One of his most powerful subjects, knowing that the king designed to take his life, appeared before him with a retinue of four hundred men, declaring that he never went abroad without that number of attendants. The tyrant had ordered a deep pit to be dug at his feet, and covered with a mat ; he desired the chief whose destruction he meditated, to seat himself on the mat, but the latter guessing the perfidious intentions of the despot, thus replied ' *Damɛl*, I am thy slave, and worthy of reposing only in the dust upon which thy feet have trod.' By this adroit answer he avoided the fate prepared for him."

The Wolof, especially the women, have a reputation for being extremely lively and cheerful. Outward behaviour, however, varies a great deal according to social position. If the daughter or wife of a chief comes on a visit, she will be accompanied by her friends, relatives, and some women of slave or *gewɛl* origin, and conversation will remain on very formal and dignified lines. Light conversation will be made by her companions, as it were, on her behalf. The low-caste groups—the smiths and the *gewɛl*—on the other hand, and to a lesser extent people of slave origin, have the utmost freedom to behave and speak as they want. The women of low-caste groups can act in an outrageously flirtatious manner, make risqué remarks, and when dancing, perform the indecent actions and postures for which Wolof dancing is notorious. As a rule high-born girls do not dance publicly or, if they do, their dancing is very restrained.

ETIQUETTE

Hands should be washed before a meal, but only the right hand is used for eating. Before beginning to eat, the eldest present gives the signal and the word *bisimilahi* is pronounced. A Wolof does not like to be watched eating by someone he does not know. There is always the fear of the " evil eye," consequently anyone nearby is invited to join. If one does not wish to eat one should say " I am satisfied " (*sur naa*), or " Thank you " (*jerejɛf*) and avoid watching the eaters.

If a stranger joins in the meal, the host may plunge his hand in the dish and stir it to cool it, as an act of politeness. The host pours on the sauce, eats the first handful, and invites his guests to follow his example. There is practically no conversation during a meal.

Women eat separately from the men. When a man is entertaining a chief or powerful man, he sends the food to his house, and does not presume to eat with him. If he is the stranger's equal, he invites him to share his calabash. When the meal is finished water is brought by the women, so that the men can drink, rinse out their mouths, rubbing their teeth with the index fingers of their right hands, and wash their hands. Women when presenting water to a man to drink should curtsey, bending down on one knee, and slightly averting the eyes.

There are numerous superstitions connected with eating—one should avoid making the dish slide, for this is believed to cause stomach ache. Wood should not be touched before washing the hands after a meal. If one happens to do so it is necessary to touch one's neck, otherwise one is liable to get a sore throat.[2]

HYGIENE

The Wolof, especially the women, use chewing sticks. Men and women bathe regularly, though perhaps not as often as the Mandinka, but their clothes are washed more frequently. However, rancid butter used in women's hairdressing gives off a distinctive odour. Hands are washed before food is taken. Only the right hand is used for eating, the left being reserved for uses inconsistent with cleanliness.

De-lousing is performed whenever the women's hair is being done. The men have their head shaved, or hair cut short. Body hair is also shaved.

[2] See Gueye, 1945, and Bodiel Thiam, 1949.

76 THE WOLOF OF SENEGAMBIA

Houses in the rural areas are only moderately clean, better than those of the Mandinka, but not so clean as those of the Fulbe or Serahuli. Various superstitious beliefs appear to play a part in this, Appia [3] mentions that to sweep out a kitchen is believed to diminish good luck. The compounds, however, are cleaner than those of the Serahuli.

On the other hand there is less overcrowding, both in the villages, and in the houses, than in other communities, and there are more beds per family. Small children often have a separate bed instead of sharing their mother's.

Water for drinking and washing is taken from deep wells, and efforts are being made to improve conditions by cementing well tops. Water pots, however, are rarely cleaned out. There is a superstition mentioned by Appia that this is not done in case the dead who come to drink find no water there. Among the Mandinka there is the belief that to clean out a water pot induces barrenness.

ENTERTAINMENTS

Dancing

More than all other Senegambian peoples one finds in the Wolof a marked sense of rhythm which constantly pervades their actions. When pounding, a woman will beat out a rhythm on the mortar with her pestle ; a smith blowing the bellows proceeds to play a tune on it ; a girl sitting idly begins to tap with her fingers on a nearby basin, and so on.

Dancing normally takes place in the evening at the *pencha* or *dat*. The spectators form a ring, with the drummers at one side. A fire is lit nearby at which the covers of the drums are heated from time to time. The *sabar* player walks about in the ring, the drummers who accompany him remain seated. The women accompany the dancing by clapping. A woman or girl enters the circle, dances for a few moments, and then returns to her place. If she is considered to have performed a particularly good dance, or is a popular girl, the women congratulate her by throwing their head-ties in the ring, or placing them round her neck, the men by giving her kola nuts or small coins. The dancer should then reward the drummer.

Aristocratic women who do not normally dance may stand in the ring with small coins in their hands to give to the drummer formally and in small amounts at regular intervals. The men may present them with further money to pass on to the drummers.

Wolof dancing is renowned for its lack of grace and the indecent actions and postures adopted by the dancers. Men—those of slave or low-caste status—dance only on special occasions such as circumcisions or weddings, or when rain and fertility dances are performed. On such occasions particularly lewd dances take place, to the great entertainment of all.

Drumming

Various types of drums (*ndenda*) are distinguished. The chief types are :—

(a) *junjuŋ*   Used only to accompany chiefs. Played with a curved stick, one hand only being used.

(b) *lamba*   A drum 70–75 cm. high ; covered with bullock skin ; beaten by the two hands.

(c) *gɔrɔŋ*   Similar to *lamba*, but smaller, 60–65 cm. high.

The *lamba* and *gɔrɔŋ* are played for minor chiefs.

(d) *sabar*   A long drum, 1 m. 12 long, of hollowed out wood, narrow in the centre, and with one end larger than the other. The end is covered with skin which is held in place by pegs. Hung round the neck of the player on the left side. Played with fingers of left hand and a stick held in the right hand.

[3] 1940, p. 377.

OTHER CULTURAL FEATURES 77

(e) *tama*	An hour-glass shaped drum, 50 cm. long, with cords joining each end. It is held under the left arm, and is played by being struck with the fingers of the left hand, and with a curved stick held in the right hand, pressure on the cords varying the tone. When playing, the drummer generally squats down on his heels.
(f) *tabala*	This drum is used for summoning people to prayer on Friday afternoon, at religious festivals, to announce a death, or give a fire alarm.
(g) Water drum	Consists of a calabash upturned in a large tin basin of water, and beaten with the two hands or two sticks. It is used only by women. Usually played when a girl is having her lips tattooed.

Lamba and *sabar* are used for wrestling matches and circumcision dances. Alarms —*njin*—notice of invasions, etc., were given by a combination of the *junjuŋ, lamba,* and *gɔrɔŋ. Junjuŋ, tama, lamba,* and *gɔrɔŋ* were played for royal festivals.

Singing

Singing and drumming are employed in co-operative working groups, setting the pace of the work, and providing distraction from the dust and the heat. On some evenings the girls hold sessions of singing, accompanied by drumming, but without dancing. The songs are led by the chief drummer (*sabarkat*), the girls joining in the chorus. Children have numerous play songs, little songs form part of children's stories ; while mothers and girls sing lullabies for their babies. Examples of these can be found in Beart.

Other Musical Instruments

Instruments used by the Wolof include guitars (*halam*), and flutes made by boys from millet stalks. As they are living in close association with the Fulbe they are also familiar with the one stringed fiddle (*riti*), and with instruments played by wandering players from other tribes—the *bɔlɔmbato*, a guitar with a skin-covered calabash as a sound box, played by the Tilibonko ; the xylophone (*balo*) played by Mandinka and Susu ; the musical bow played by Jola and Futa Toro Fulbe.

Wrestling

Wrestling is the favourite sport of all the Senegal peoples. The main wrestling season is held from harvest time (about October) until the trade season (December– January, when the groundnuts are sold). Intervillage competitions are held. A general account of wrestlers and their preparations for competitions is given by Gorer,[4] while the various holds are described by Balandier.[5] To European eyes the wrestling is rather dull, for more time is devoted to preparing for contests than to the actual wrestling, and one needs to be brought up in the culture to appreciate its finer points.

Play-acting

Occasionally one may see play-acting performed by a troupe of wandering players ; biting caricatures, short, cleverly performed sketches, becoming more indecent as the evening wears on.

Miscellaneous Games

A detailed study of West African games has been made by Beart who describes among others nearly 500 Wolof games. The principal games of young men include

[4] 1935, pp. 27–32.
[5] 1952, p. 60.

78   THE WOLOF OF SENEGAMBIA

wuri, a game played with counters placed in a series of holes (six holes a side in a wooden block with two larger containers at each end) ; *yɔtɛ*, like draughts, but using sticks stuck into ridges in the sand ; *ndal*, similar to draughts but with a larger board than the English version ; and various modern games, *marias*, a card game (from French mariage ?) and *kuta*, a gambling game played by tossing a matchbox.

Children imitate adult festivities such as weddings. They build houses of wet sand. Girls have dolls, in the simplest form a large bone, in more elaborate forms stuffed dolls with wool hair fastened on, which they carry around on their backs. They " cook " food in old tins, and practise pounding. Small boys make lorries of raphia-palm wood which they pull around on strings. They ride hobby-horses of millet stalks. They play with hoops, old bicycle wheels operated by a string tied to the wheel and to a piece of stick. They make flutes from millet stalks.

In urban centres various forms of hopscotch, presumably introduced from Europe, are the current rage among the girls, while small boys play football and " tennis "—using for the latter wooden bats like table tennis bats. Older girls devote much time to ludo.

Horsemanship

In earlier times the Wolof were renowned for their skill in horsemanship. Marmol describing the visit of a Wolof Prince Bemoy to Portugal in 1481, says : " He had with him people very skilful on horseback who rode standing upright on the saddle, and while in motion, sat down, and stood up again, jumped to the ground with their hands on the saddle, and mounted again, as if they had been standing still, and picked up from the ground as they rode stones which were thrown to them, and other skilful actions . . . "

Moore (1735) writes of a Wolof chief, " I have seen him do wonders upon this horse, sometimes making him advance 40 or 50 yards together on his two hinder feet, without touching the ground with his fore ones, sometimes curvetting round a ring, and then straining him so low with his belly to the ground as to carry him under the Mundingo penthouses, which are not above four foot high." Adanson (1752) tells of the horsemanship seen at the festival of Tabaski . . . " they raised their feet, and touched the ground lightly and in cadence ; all the movements of their bodies exactly accorded with the sound of the instruments ; in a word, their gestures bore a perfect resemblance to a most regular dance . . . the horsemen . . . managed their horses, and made them imitate whatever they pleased, feigning by their gesture and attitude, sometimes a combat, and other times a justling, a chace, or dance."

At the present day with the growth of modern transport, few horses are to be seen in Wolof country, though most Wolof chiefs still keep horses which they use when travelling in their districts, and which, to a certain extent, are a sign of their high position.

Lanterns

A special form of entertainment, found in urban centres, especially at Christmas and the New Year, is the parade of lanterns (*fanal*) through the streets. These are made from paper and wood in the form of ships, houses, motors, etc., lit by candles, and vary from those less than a foot in size, made by small boys, to ships over six feet long carried on a framework by four men. An association is often formed to contribute to the costs of making the lantern—many weeks work are often involved and great skill and ingenuity is displayed in the workmanship—and at the appropriate time they are carried round and shown to prominent members of the community who are expected to make a contribution. In Senegal the parades of lanterns became involved in political clashes and were banned in 1954, but lanterns are still made in Bathurst, and Gambian trading centres with a large Wolof population.

CHANGING SOCIAL CONDITIONS

One of the characteristics of the Wolof is that from earliest times they have shown themselves extremely adaptable and taken over from those with whom they were in contact—Portuguese, French, English, Mauretanians, Futa Toro Fulbe, Lebanese, etc., new skills and ideas which enabled them to occupy and hold leading positions in relation to neighbouring peoples. They showed none of the anti-French attitude displayed by the Mauretanians and Futa Toro Fulbe, and French expansion into the interior owed a lot to Wolof and Lebu soldiers, sailors, and interpreters.

Even in the days of the slave trade a premium was paid for Wolof slaves who were found to be more suitable as household servants than as plantation workers. Pruneau de Pommegorge wrote that the Wolof women learnt with the greatest ease, so that a few months after their arrival in the American colonies they could sew, speak French, and serve as well as European domestic servants, often becoming chamber maids to the Creole ladies.

Gorer writes : " They generally adapt themselves very well to changed conditions, and nearly all positions which require intellectual training and independence—such as auxiliary doctors, midwives, clerks to the administrations, storekeepers—are filled by Wolof in French Guinea, French Soudan and the Ivory Coast."

In the early days of Bathurst, the Wolof played an important part in the establishment and development of the town. The early settlers and traders, who had formerly been at Gorée, but withdrew to Bathurst when that island was restored to the French, brought with them their Wolof families for they had been " as much disposed to submit to the Jaloff charms, as had been their predecessors the French . . . " " Many of the offspring of these alliances were affectionately reared by their parents, some of them receiving good education in England, and others marrying highly respectable residents among the English society of the place . . . the Jaloff was found actively engaged in the business of the merchant, assiduous as an employee under the government, and industrious as a tradesman. Many of them were officers in the corps called " Royal Gambia Militia," and the lieut.-colonel of that force was selected by the governor from this class of the inhabitants . . . " (Huntley 1851). The Wolof then played a great part in commerce, many owning shops in Bathurst and trading vessels which travelled up river. The dominant position in trade has now been taken from the Wolof by the Lebanese, though the majority of shopkeepers working under them are still Wolof.

In the Senegal the Wolof showed the ability to profit from European education. Dard wrote " from 1818 to 1820, several Wolof, in less than four years, have learnt French, the elements of geography, mathematics, physics, chemistry, natural history, and navigation." On the other hand, it is only in comparatively recent times in the Gambia that the Wolof have taken to European studies—formerly the concentration was on Arabic studies. Morgan writing in 1864 stated : " Next to the Moors they are the best Arabic scholars, and better acquainted with the Koran than others. . . . Some of the Jaloofs wrote Arabic in beautiful characters ; could read the Arabic Bible well, and, as they read, translate into their own tongue . . . "

European education in Bathurst was largely in the hands of the Missions and most of those who taught were Aku or Creole Christians. The result was that few Muslims sent their children to school, and there had come into being a clerical class of Akus holding the majority of positions in Government Service and in the commercial firms.[1] In the Gambia Government Staff List for 1935, 80% of the clerks had Aku (" European ") names. In recent years the picture has changed. A much greater proportion of the Wolof has been attending school, and educated Wolof are now gradually taking over positions formerly the virtual monopoly of the Aku.

Change has undoubtedly become more rapid in all spheres of life in the past ten years. Though Wolof dress is unmistakable, a study of old photographs shows many

---

[1] Annual Report on the Education Department for the years 1947, 1948, and 1949. Sessional Paper No. 8/52.

80　　　　　　　THE WOLOF OF SENEGAMBIA

changes in dress and hair style. Gambians say that St. Louis copies Paris fashions, Dakar copies St. Louis, while Bathurst copies Dakar. In Dakar elegant Wolof have been chosen as mannequins, and are provided with free dresses, in order to stimulate interest in new styles. The result is that fashions are said to change every six months instead of every two years. Dressmakers in the Gambia often study with keen interest women's magazines containing illustrations of dresses and incorporate various features, types of sleeves, necklines, etc., in their own creations, though the final result is unmistakably African. Accessories, too, are subject to change. More and more women wear imported plastic sandals instead of those locally made, keep their money in purses, and when going to market carry European made shopping bags instead of calabashes. Plastic raincoats are in common use. Nail varnish is used as well as henna.

In urban centres the custom of shaving the hair of girls into various patterns has largely died out and school uniforms have taken the place of native dress during school hours. European type clothing is generally worn by men employed in clerical jobs or in shops, etc., though native robes are put on for the Friday afternoon prayer or religious festivals.

Traditional games are giving way to modern entertainments. The sale of small short wave battery radio sets has meant that the influence of radio now reaches beyond urban zones. Appreciation of the cinema is growing, Tarzan, Charlie Chaplin, and news reels showing horse racing being among the most popular items, though the younger generation prefer cowboys. Fewer people play *wuri*—the men play cards, young women ludo. Various forms of hopscotch are played by small girls ; boys play football and " tennis," while football and cycle racing are becoming increasingly popular among the young men.

In urban centres the growth of political parties has provided a new interest in life. Politicians provide drummers and *gewel* to enliven their electioneering campaigns.

Life in the towns has provided a greater degree of emancipation for women. In the Senegal the girls attend school, speak French, and afterwards look for positions which will enable them to live an independent life. They have greater freedom of choice in marriage ; can go out on their own, attend European type dances, and dress according to their own tastes. Among highly educated classes polygamy is becoming rarer.[2]

The Wolof women, more than other peoples, have taken to modern means of transportation. In the Gambia when visiting the Kombo region they ride in local taxis in preference to the lorries which are converted into buses. In Dakar many go to market in horse drawn vehicles. The modern Wolof girl in Bathurst often rides a bicycle, a sight causing many an old Mandinka or Jola to exclaim in horror that the world is completely spoilt now, though in Dakar emancipation has progressed so far that girls are to be seen riding pillion on motor scooters.

Life in urban centres is also associated with a decline in morals. The rising cost of living, high marriage expenses, and housing difficulties have meant later marriages for both men and women. Homosexuality, practically unknown in rural society, has become established in large towns. Prostitution exists in the ports and big trade centres.

[2] Diagne (1947).

BIBLIOGRAPHY OF LINGUISTIC MATERIAL

VOCABULARIES, DICTIONARIES, GRAMMARS, ETC.

Books or articles which I have not personally seen are marked after the author's name with the source from which the title was obtained:

(a) Joucla (E.). *Bibliographie de l'Afrique Occidentale Française.* (1937.)

(b) de Tressan (M. de L.). *Inventaire Linguistique de l'Afrique Occidentale Française et du Togo.* (1953.)

(c) Library Catalogue. IFAN. Dakar.

1732 Barbot, J.
A Description of the Coasts of North & South Guinea, etc. (Pp. 413–20. Gives the numerals, 27 short sentences, and a vocabulary of about 200 words.)

1745 Astley, Thomas
Voyages and Travels, etc. (Vol. II, pp. 290–3. Repeats Barbot's vocabulary, etc)

1789 Pommegorge, Pruneau de
Description de la Nigritie. (Pp. 278–84. Short list of Wolof words, the numerals, and some phrases.)

1802 Golberry, S. M. X.
Fragmens d'un Voyage en Afrique. (Vol. II, chap. XVIII, pp. 132–47. Contains about 170 words and phrases.)

1807 Corry, J.
Observations upon the Windward Coast of Africa, etc. (Pp. 159–62. Vocabulary of about 100 words and phrases.)

1814 R. G. V. (Geoffroy de Villeneuve)
L'Afrique, ou histoire, moeurs, usages, et coutumes des Africains. Le Sénégal. (Vocabulaire de la langue ouolofe—25 pages—at the end of vol. I.)

1820 Mollien, G.
Travels in the Interior of Africa to the sources of the Senegal and Gambia. . . . (Pp. 372–8—Wolof vocabulary.)

1820 Mrs. Kilham (published anonymously)
Ta-re Wa-loof, Ta-re boo Juk-à. First lessons in Jaloff.

1823 Mrs. Kilham (published anonymously)
African Lessons, Wolof and English, in three parts. (1) Easy lessons, and narratives for schools; (2) Examples in Grammar, Family Advices, Short Vocabulary; (3) Selections from the Holy Scriptures.

Undated (probably about 1830) Mrs. Kilham (published anonymously)
Thirty sheets of African language lessons. (This was an early attempt at mass education. It includes a Wolof sheet.)
The works of Mrs. Kilham are to be found in the library of the Society of Friends, London.

1825 Dard, J.
Dictionnaire français-wolof et français-bambara, suivi du dictionnaire wolof-français.

1826 Dard, J.
Grammaire Wolofe ou méthode pour étudier la langue des noirs, etc. . . .

1829 Roger, Baron
Recherches philosophiques sur la langue ouolofe suivies d'un vocabulaire abrégé français-ouolof.

1842 Lambert, M. (b)
Grammaire Ouolove, précédé d'une introduction intitulée : Les Ouolofs par M. A. Renzé.

1845 (Edited by M. d'Avezac)
" Vocabulaires Guiolof, Mandingue, Foule, Saracole, Seraire, Bagnon et Floupe, recueillis à la Côte d'Afrique pour le service de l'ancienne Compagnie Royale du Sénégal (d'après un manuscrit de la Bibliothèque Royale)." *Mémoires de la Société ethnologique,* pp. 207–67.
(Many errors were made in transcribing from the original manuscript.)

1855 Kobès, Mgr. A. (a)
Dictionnaire français-wolof.

1856 Kobès, Mgr. A. (a)
Principes de la langue wolofe.

1858 Boilat, Abbé
Grammaire de la langue woloffe.

1864 Faidherbe, L.
Vocabulaire d'environ 1,500 mots français avec leur correspondants en Ouolof de Saint Louis . . . etc.

81

F

82 THE WOLOF OF SENEGAMBIA

1864 Descemet, L.
Recueil d'environ 1,200 phrases françaises usuelles avec leur traduction en regard en Ouolof de Saint-Louis.

1867 Kobès, Mgr. A.
Grammaire de la langue volofe.

1873 Kobès, Mgr. A. (b)
Dictionnaire volof-français, précédé d'un abrégé de grammaire.

1875 (Missionaires de la Mission de Sénégambie.) (a)
Dictionnaire wolof-français (précédé d'un abrégé de grammaire wolofe). (Same as item above?)

1875 Faidherbe, L.
Essai sur la langue Poul. ... (Pp. 67–78 for a comparison between Wolof, Serer, and Poul, i.e., Fula.)

1875 —— (a)
Dictionnaire français-wolof et wolof-français.

1878 Fieldhouse, Rev. J.
Grammar of the Jolof Language. (Wesleyan Missionary Society, London.)

1880 ——
Guide de la conversation en quatre langues: français, volof, anglais, sérèr. (Saint Joseph de N'Gazobil.)
(Contains word lists, the conjugations of verbs, and conversational sentences.)

1887 Faidherbe, Le Général.
Langues Sénégalaises. Wolof, Arabe-Hassania, Soninké, Sérère.
(Notions Grammaticales, pp. 5–23; Vocabulaires, pp. 73–169; et Phrases, pp. 207–47.)

1888 Speisser, F. L.
Grammaire élémentaire de la langue voloffe.

1890 Poussié, Dr. E. (a)
Manuel de conversation en trente langues ... (includes wolof).

1890 Guy-Grand, V.-J.
Dictionnaire Français-Volof. (3rd edition), *revue et considérablement augmentée.*

1898 Rambaud, J. B. (a)
" La détermination en wolof." *Bul. de la Soc. de Linguistique de Paris,* pp. 122–36.

1902 (Missionaires de la Congregation du Saint-Esprit et du Coeur de Marie).
Dictionnaire Volof-français précédé d'un abrégé de la grammaire volofe.

1903 Rambaud, J. B.
La langue wolof.
(A study of Saint-Louis Wolof. Wolof grammar, pp. 1–52; French-Wolof vocabulary, pp. 53–106.)

1905 Graner, (a)
Manuel de conversation wolof-française.

no date ——
Guide de la conversation Français-Volof. (Mission Catholique, Dakar.)

1907 (PP. du Saint-Esprit).
Guide de conversation français-wolof-diola-serrer.

1912 Homburger, Mlle. L.
" Le Wolof et les parlers bantous." *Mémoires de la Société de Linguistique de Paris,* XVII, pp. 311–36.

1912 Reeve, H. F.
The Gambia. (List of birds, mammals, reptiles, fishes, and insects given by Dr. E. Hopkinson, pp. 277–82.)

1923 Kobès, Mgr. A.
Dictionnaire Volof-Français. (Nouvelle édition par le R. P. O. Abiven.)

1923 Guy-Grand, V.-J.
Dictionnaire Français-Volof, précédé d'un abrégé de la grammaire volofe. (Nouvelle édition ... par le R. P. O. Abiven.)

1924 —— (c)
Syllabaire Volof. (Dakar. Impr. de la Mission.)

1927 Delafosse, M.
" Les classes nominales en wolof." *Festscrift Meinhof,* Hambourg, pp. 29–44.

1934 Lo, Adama
Bindou ouolofel ti arafou toubab. (Méthode d'écriture de la langue Ouolof en lettres latines.)
(An introduction to writing for children not attending school.)

1934 Labouret, H.
Remarques sur la langue des Wolof. In " Pêcheurs de Guet N'Dar." *Bull. de Comité d'Études Hist. et Scientifiques de l'A.O.F* T.XVII, No. 2, pp. 288–95.

1939 Ward, Ida C.
" A short phonetic study of Wolof (Jolof) as spoken in the Gambia and in Senegal." *Africa,* vol. XII, No. 3, July, pp. 320–34.

BIBLIOGRAPHIES

1940 Mouradian, J.
" Note sur quelque emprunts de la langue wolof à l'arabe." *Bull. IFAN*, 2 3/4, pp. 269–84.
1943 Angrand, A.-P.
Manuel Français-Ouolof. (Dakar.)
(This is one of the few available works on Wolof. Though containing some useful word lists, an inconsistent and non-phonetic system of spelling is used, while grammatical notes are extremely scanty.)
1943 Senghor, L. S.
" Les classes nominales en Wolof et les substantifs à initiale nasale." *J. Soc. Afric.*, XIII, pp. 109–22.
1947 Senghor, L. S.
" L'article conjonctif en wolof." *J. Soc. Afric.*, XVII, pp. 19–22.
1947 Badiane, D. M.
" Quelque mots à ne pas confondre en wolof." *Notes Africaines*, 34, p. 19.
1948 Diop, Cheikh Anta
" Études de linguistique ouolove." *Présence Africaine* 4, pp. 672–84. *Présence Africaine* 5, pp. 848–53.
1949 Ndiaye, Aissetou
" Complément à une note sur quelques emprunts de la langue wolof à l'arabe." *Notes Africaines* 41. pp. 22–9.
1951 Sissoko, F. D.
" Emprunts de mots au Soudan Français." *Conf. Intern. des Afric. de l'Ouest.* Tome II, pp. 216–23.
1952 Gouilly, A.
L'Islam dans l'Afrique Occidentale Française. (Ch. IX, pp. 207–20 for words borrowed from Arabic.)
1952 Société de Linguistique de Paris
Les langues du monde, pp. 834–40.
1952 Westermann, D., and Bryan, M. A.
Handbook of African Languages. Part II. Languages of West Africa.
1953 de Tressan, M. de L.
Inventaire Linguistique de l'Afrique Occidentale Française et du Togo. Mem. IFAN, No. 30, 1953, pp. 146–60.

RELIGIOUS LITERATURE [1]

ROMAN CATHOLIC MISSIONS   I

1878 (St. Joseph de Ngasobil)
Bibal bu tuti bu anda'k i natal. (Illustrated. Biblical extracts.)
1881 (St. Joseph de Ngasobil)
Nroy um Yésu-Krista. (Translation of " L'imitation de Jésus Christ.")
Undated
Habar u Voleri gu ditu ga. (Illustrated Bible.)
1914 ———
Voy yu sela (yu no voy ṭi Vicaria apostolik u Sénégambi), pp. 138. Dakar. Impr. de la Mission.
(Hymn-book, Prayers and the Stations of the Cross.)
1922 (Mission Catholique, Dakar)
Katésism m'ba ndemantalé yon u Katolik (Volof), pp. 138.
(Prayers, Catechism, Description of the Sacraments, Confession, Mass, etc.)
1925 ———
Tabi aldana (mba téré ñan ak voy ak ada ndulit yi ño ubil bunt'u Aldana). Dakar. Impr. de la Mission.
(Missal in Wolof. Prayers, Hymns, Stations of the Cross, etc.)
1930 (Fathers of the Congregation of the Holy Ghost, Bathurst)
Voy u Katolik. (A hymn-book.)

[1] For over a hundred years the Roman Catholic Missionaries, especially those of the Mission of St. Joseph de Ngasobil, have prepared translations of catechisms, hymn-books, Bible translations, and other devotional works of which it has proved impossible to prepare a reliable bibliography for a number of reasons. In bibliographies and catalogues the titles have often been copied inaccurately. Sometimes the title is given in Wolof, sometimes in French, making it difficult to decide whether there are two works or one. When an edition has become exhausted, revisions, corrections, and changes in the orthography are often made before a second is issued. Without seeing the works in question, one cannot tell whether one is dealing with a second printing, or a new work. Many of the books bear no date.
    In compiling the lists below I have therefore first of all given those books which I have seen myself (I) and a second list (II) of those which it has not been possible to check.

F2

84 THE WOLOF OF SENEGAMBIA

1934 R. P. Jeuland and M. Jacques Bill
      Martir u Luganda ya. (Les martyrs de l'Ouganda. Traduction volofe de l'opuscule de
      Mgr. Streicher.)
1943 (Mission Catholique, Dakar)
      Katesism mba ndyemantale yon u Katolik.

II

In 1880 the Mission of St. Joseph de Ngasobil sold :
1. *Épîtres et Évangiles de tous les dimanches de l'année en volof.*
2. *Catéchisme des colonies en volof.*
3. *Catéchisme Volof pour les adultes, le Français en regard.*
4. *Chemin de la Croix, Volof.*
5. *Cantiques Volofs.*
6. *Manuel de piété sous le titre de Tabi Aldana, à l'usage des chrétiens du Vicariat apostolique de la Sénégambie.*
7. *Bible illustrée en Volof.*
8. *Alphabet Volof.*

Additional works mentioned in Joucla : *Bibliographie de l'A.O.F.* are :

1843 Lambert, Abbé
      Grand Catéchisme Wolof.
1848 Missions de la Guinée
      Ave Maria en Wolof. (Ann. de la Propagat. de la Foi., XX, 313.)
1854 Kobès, Mgr. A.
      Catéchisme pour les enfants. Texte wolof.
1855 Kobès, Mgr. A.
      Évangiles pour les dimanches et fêtes en Wolof.
1862 Kobès, Mgr. A.
      Catéchisme Français-Wolof pour les adultes.
1878 Lacombe, Le. P.
      Traduction en wolof du catéchisme des colonies françaises, approuvée par la Propagande.
1886 Anon. (St. Joseph de N'Gazobil)
      Catéchisme (Nouveau), texte wolof.
1893 Anon.
      Catéchisme en français et en wolof à l'usage du provicariat de la Sénégambie et de la préfecture du Sénégal.
1922 Anon.
      Katésism bu anda'k natal am.

METHODIST MISSIONS

1878 Fieldhouse, Rev. James
      Joloff Primer.
Undated, probably *c.* 1878   (Wesleyan Missionary Society.)
      I nan ce Joluf, 8 pp.   (Prayers in Wolof.)
Undated, probably *c.* 1908   (Methodist Publishing House, London.)
      Katekism i Wesleyan Methodist yi chi gune yi. (A Catechism for children.)
1908 ———
      Voy yu sela. (A hymn-book.)
1909 ———
      Tere bu yomba chi yon i kerchen. (A primer of Christian doctrine.)

Round about 1907 the Rev. R. Dixon translated several of the gospels into Wolof. Translations of St. John and St. Matthew were published by the British and Foreign Bible Society. The MSS of the translation of St. Mark is to be found at the Methodist Mission, Bathurst.

1907 ———
      St. John in Jolof.
1935 ———
      St. Matthew in Jolof. (*Linjil i Yesu Krista.*)

ISLAMIC SECTS

1954 (Bahá'í Publishing Trust.)
      Dinna Bahd'í : Modi dine nyu japante.

BIBLIOGRAPHIES

MISCELLANEOUS

Items which it has not been possible to check are :
1874   (Soc. Bibl. de France)
       L'évangile selon Saint Jean en Wolof.   (*Evansil naka Yoana mou sèla ma.*)
                (Source : Library Catalogue.   IFAN.   Dakar.)
1904   (Société des Missions Évangéliques chez les peuples non Chrétiens)
       Voy yalla ndah dangou lindil.   (Senegal hymns.)
                (Source : *Bibliography of African Christian Literature.*   1923.)
1922   Romarch
       Recueil de morceaux religieux et profanes en langue wolof.
                (Source : Library Catalogue.   I.A.I.   London.)

GENERAL BIBLIOGRAPHY

As the Wolof have long been in contact with Europeans, references to them in Senegambian literature are numerous.   Often, however, in general descriptions of the Senegal (e.g. Richard-Molard), in the memoirs of missionaries (Fox, Moister, Morgan), in the accounts of travellers who merely passed through their territory on the way into the interior (Park, Caillié, Soleillet, etc.) or in the writings of tourists old and new (F. R. G. S., Gaunt, Hardinge, Huxley, Mills, Mitchinson, Rankin), only the briefest mention of the Wolof has been made though often facts of interest or vivid descriptive pieces have been given.   In the bibliography all the pages in such works which refer to the Wolof have been noted.   In the case of books provided with an index, and those in which references to the Wolof are numerous (Adanson, Cultru, Golberry, Mollien, etc.), full page references are not given.

Adanson, M.
   1759   *A voyage to Senegal, the Isle of Gorée, and the River Gambia.*   (1749–53.)
Ames, D. W.
   1955   " The economic base of Wolof polygyny."   *Southwestern Journal of Anthropology.*
                Vol.II, No. 4, pp. 391–403.
   1955   " Wolof music of Senegal and the Gambia."   (Gramophone record and descriptive
                article.   Ethnic Folkways Library Album, P. 462.   New York.)
   1955   " The use of a transitional cloth-money token among the Wolof."   *American Anthro-
                pologist.* Vol. 57, No. 5, pp. 1016–24.
   1956   " The selection of mates, courtship and marriage among the Wolof."   *Bull. IFAN.*,
                T. XVIII, Nos. 1–2, pp. 156–68.
Anderson, J. N. D.
   1954   *Islamic Law in Africa.*
                (Gambia, pp. 225–48.   Contains an account of Bathurst Wolof marriage procedure.)
Angrand, A.-P.
   1943   *Manuel Français-Ouolof.*
                (Proverbs, etc., pp. 74–5, 78 ; legends, p. 74.)
Anon.
   1885   *Annales Sénégalaises de 1854 à 1885 suivies des traités passés avec les indigènes.*   (Details
                of French military expeditions in Senegal.)
Anon.
   1946   " Calendrier Agricole pour le Sénégal."   *Bull. IFAN.*, pp. 138–63.
                (Covers the Wolof area—Jolof, Walo, pp. 141–8 ;   Kayor, Baol and Sine-Salum,
                      pp. 148–56.)
Appia, Béatrice
   1940   " Superstitions Guinéennes et Sénégalaises."   *Bull. IFAN.*, pp. 376–82.
                (A list of about a hundred miscellaneous beliefs.)
Appia-Dabit, Béatrice
   1943   " Notes sur quelques bijoux sénégalais."   *Bull. IFAN.*, pp. 27–30.
                (Descriptions and illustrations of jewellery.)
Astley, Thomas
   1745   *A new general collection of voyages and travels.* . . . Vols. I and II.
                (A valuable source book for old material—Cada Mosto, Labat, Barbot, Jannequin,
                      de Rochefort, Le Maire, etc., the originals of which are rarely available.)
Aujas, L.
   1925   " Funérailles royales et ordre de succession au trône chez les Sérères du Sine."   *Bull.
                du Com. d'Études Hist. et Scient. de l'A.O.F.*, pp. 501–8.
                (Describes the procedure at the death of a *bur*, the order of succession, and provides
                      a list of the rulers of Sine.)
   1931   " Les Sérères du Sénégal (Moeurs et Coutumes de droit privé)."   *Bull. du. Com.
                d'Études Hist. et Scient. de l'A.O.F.*, juil-sept., T. XIV, No. 3, pp. 293–333.
                (Useful for comparative purposes.)

86 THE WOLOF OF SENEGAMBIA

Badiane, D. M.
1948 " L'interpellation nocturne chez les Wolofs." *Notes Africaines*, oct., p. 17.
Balandier, G.
1949 " Femmes ' possédées ' et leurs chants." *Présence Africaine*, 5, pp. 749–54.
(Refers to the Lebu.)
Balandier, G., and Mercier, P.
1952 *Les Pêcheurs Lebou.*
Barbot, J.
1732 *A Description of the Coasts of North and South Guinea*, etc. Edition of 1732.
(The first edition seems to have been prepared about 1682.)
Bardon, P.
1949 " Le Ouolof." *Tropiques*, 47, dec., pp. 42–4.
(A brief and simple summary of the Wolof " caste " system.)
Basset, R.
1903 *Contes populaires d'Afrique.*
(Contains translations of two Wolof stories (pp. 182–5) taken from Boilat's *Grammaire* etc., of 1858.)
Beart, Ch.
1955 *Jeux et jouets de l'ouest africain. IFAN.*, 2 vols.
Bérenger-Féraud, L.-J.-B.
1879 *Les Peuplades de la Sénégambie*, pp. 1–62.
(An early ethnographic survey.)
1885 *Recueil de contes populaires de la Sénégambie.*
(These stories are also given in *Les Peuplades de la Sénégambie.*)
Bessac, H.
1953 " Contribution à l'étude des buttes à coquillages du Saloum (Sénégal)." *Notes Africaines*, No. 57, pp. 1–4.
(A study of shell heaps in the Salum region.)
Biller, Sarah
1837 *Memoir of Hannah Kilham*, pp. 132–3, 169, 189, 193, 197–8.
(Mrs. Kilham was one of the first missionary teachers in the Gambia. She began studying Wolof and preparing schoolbooks in London in 1820, and went to the Gambia in 1823.)
Blake, J. W.
1942 *Europeans in West Africa*, 1450–1560, pp. 32, 80–6.
(Gives details of the visit of a Wolof prince to Portugal in the 1480s.)
Boilat, L'Abbé P. D.
1853 *Esquisses Sénégalaises.*
Bourgeau, J.
1933 " Notes sur la coutume des Sérères du Sine et du Saloum." *Bull. du Com. d'Études Hist. et Scient. de l'A.O.F.*, T. XVI, No. 1, jan.-mar., pp. 1–65.
(Useful for comparison.)
Bowdich, T. E.
1825 *Excursions in Madeira and Porto Santo, to which is added.* . . . " *A description of the English settlements on the River Gambia*," by Mrs. Bowdich, pp. 207–10.
Brasseur, G.
1952 *Le problème de l'eau au Senegal. IFAN.*
Burton, R. F.
1865 *Wit and Wisdom from West Africa*, pp. 3–37.
(A list of proverbs taken from Dard's grammar.)
Caillié, R.
1830 *Travels through Central Africa to Timbuctoo*, vol. I, pp. 6, 31.
(Contains description of fishing with nets in Walo.)
Campistron, M.
1939 " Coutume Ouolof du Cayor (Cercle de Thiès)," in *Coutumiers juridiques de l'Afrique Occidentale Française.* T. I, Sénégal, pp. 117–46.
Cendrars, Blaise
1947 *Anthologie nègre.*
(Contains three Wolof stories—nos. 74, 79, and 106.)
Chabas, J.
1952 " Le mariage et le divorce dans les coutumes des Ouolofs habitant les grands centres du Sénégal." *Revue Juridique et Politique de l'Union Française*, No. 4, oct.-dec., pp. 474–532.
(An extremely useful study of Wolof marriage law.)
1956 " Le droit des successions chez les Ouolofs." *Annales Africaines*, No. 1, pp. 75–119.
(A detailed study of inheritance.)
Cultru, P.
1913 *Premier Voyage du Sieur de la Courbe fait à la coste d'Afrique en 1685.*
(This account was copied and enlarged by Labat.)

BIBLIOGRAPHIES

87

Dapper, D'O.
1686   *Description de l'Afrique.* Amsterdam.
De la Courbe—*see* Cultru
Delafosse, M.
1922   *L'Ame nègre.*
. (Contains proverbs, riddles, and stories taken from Boilat and Baron Roger.)
Demaison, A.
1931   *Diaeli, le livre de la sagesse noire.*
(Contains translations of stories and proverbs from Mandinka and Wolof sources
without, however, saying which are which. The majority appear to be Wolof.)
Diagne, A. M.
1919   " Un pays de pilleurs d'épaves : Le Gandiole." *Bull. du Com. d'Études Hist. et Scient.*
de l'A.O.F., pp. 137–76.
(After outlining the boundaries, natural regions, economic life, political organiza-
tion, and legends of origin, deals with the rights claimed over shipwrecks,
the disputes with the French concerning them, and the gradual extension of
French influence.)
Diagne, O. S.
1947   " Les frais du mariage Saint-Louisien, origines, principaux aspects et consequences."
Notes Africaines, avr., pp. 8–13.
(Discusses rising cost of marriage in urban centres.)
Diakhate, Lamine
1955   " M'Baye Rab Gueye. Poète et penseur sénégalais d'expression ouolove." *Présence*
Africaine, 4, oct.-nov., pp. 76–80.
(An appreciation of a modern Wolof poet.)
Diop, Cheikh Anta
1948   " Études de linguistique ouolove." *Présence Africaine,* 4, pp. 672–84.
" Origines de la langue et de la race valaf." *Présence Africaine,* 5, pp. 848–53.
(His views should be regarded with a critical eye.)
Duchemin, Cap.
1906   Tumulus de la Gambie. *Bull. et Mém. de la Soc. d'Anthrop. de Paris,* pp. 25–34.
Durand, J. P. L.
1806   *A voyage to Senegal.*
(Durand mentions that all his papers were lost in a shipwreck. The book was
clearly written with assistance from previous writings on the Senegal.)
Equilbecq, F. V.
1915   *Contes Indigènes et l'Ouest Africain Français,* vol. II.
(Wolof stories are Nos. XX, XXIX, XXXVII, LVI, LX.)
Ellis, A. B.
1883   *The Land of Fetish.* Ch. I.
(Superficial remarks by a military officer stationed for a short time in the Gambia.)
Faidherbe, Le Général
1883   " Notice historique sur le Cayor." *Bull. Soc. Géog. de Paris,* T. IV, pp. 527–64.
Fayet, M. J. C.
1939   " Coutume des Ouolof musulmans (Cercle du Baol)," in *Coutumiers Juridiques de*
l'Afrique Occidentale Français. T. I, Sénégal, pp. 147–93.
Fernandes—*see* Monod.
Findlay, G. G., and Holdsworth, W. W.
1921   *The History of the Wesleyan Methodist Missionary Society,* vol. IV, chap. II, The
Gambia, p. 141.
(Mentions translation of gospels, hymns, etc., into Wolof by Rev. Robert Dixon,
1905–09.)
Forde, C. Daryll
1945   *Report on need for ethnographic and sociological research in the Gambia,* pp. 5, 11.
Fox, William
1851   *A brief history of the Wesleyan Missions on the Western Coast of Africa,* pp. 236, 359, 475.
Frey, Le Colonel
1890   *Côte Occidentale d'Afrique.*
(The text contains little of interest, but there are over 20 diagrams showing
Wolof dress, dancing, etc., many being of the " signares " of Saint Louis.)
F. R. G. S.
1863   *Wanderings in West Africa from Liverpool to Fernando Po.,* vol. I, chap. IV, pp. 152, 154.
(A tourist's account.)
Gaden, H.
1912   " Légendes et coutumes Sénégalaises. Cahiers de Yoro Dyao." *Rev. d'Eth. et de*
Sociologie, pp. 119–37 and 191–202.
(Notes on Yoro Dyao and an account of the origin of the Wolof Empire and the
legend of Ndyadyane Ndyaye ; description of the election of rulers in the six
Wolof states, giving a very detailed account of ceremonies in Walo.)

88 THE WOLOF OF SENEGAMBIA

1914   *Le Poular.*
     (See pp. 327–32 for an account of secret languages in Fula and Wolof, etc.)

Gamble, D. P.
1949   *Contributions to a Socio-Economic Survey of the Gambia.* Colonial Office.
     (Account of Wolof agriculture and details of income and expenditure in a Wolof community.)
1952   " Infant mortality rates in rural areas in the Gambia Protectorate." *Jour. of Trop. Med. & Hyg.*, July. pp. 145–49.
     (Includes data for a Wolof village.)

Gaunt, Mary
1912   *Alone in West Africa*, chap. II, The Gambia.

Gaye, Th. M.
1944   " À propos des ' Javanais ' ouest-africains." *Notes Africaines*, juin, p. 3.
     (An account of secret languages.)

Golberry, S. M. X.
1802   *Fragmens d'un voyage en Afrique* (1785–87). 2 vols.

Gorer, G.
1935   *Africa Dances.* Penguin edition, pp. 9–40, 51.
     (A rather journalistic account of the Wolof, with some errors of detail, yet containing many highly illuminating remarks on the Wolof.)

Gouilly, A.
1952   *L'Islam dans l'Afrique Occidentale Française.*

Gray, J. M.
1940   *A history of the Gambia.*
     (Contains nothing original on the Wolof.)

Gravier, G.
1887   *Paul Soleillet—Voyage à Segou* (1878–1879).
     (P. 136 mentions the iler, the introduction of which he attributes to Hilaire Maurel. But see Richard-Molard, 1950 ; p. 142, origin of the title *Brak* of Walo.)

Gray, W., and Dochard
1825   *Travels in Western Africa* (1818–21). . . . Pp. 46, 192–3.

Gueye, Mody
1945   " Quèlques Habitudes des Wolofs." *Notes Africaines*, juillet, p. 21.
     (Miscellaneous superstitions connected with eating and travelling.)

Guillot, R.
1933   " Contes d'Afriques." *Numéro spécial du Bulletin de l'Enseignement de l'A.O.F.*
     (Contains about 20 Wolof stories.)

Hamlyn, W. T.
1931   *A short history of the Gambia.* Bathurst, pp. 16–17, 18–19.
     (An elementary schoolbook, revised as " Stories of the Gambia," 1945.)

Hardinge, R.
1934   *Gambia and Beyond*, pp. 18, 51, 160.
     (A traveller who passed through the Gambia.)

Hauser, A.
1954   " Les industries de transformation de la région de Dakar." In *Études Sénégalaises* No. 5.
     (An outline of industrialization in the Dakar region.)

Hecquard, H.
1855   *Voyages sur la côte et dans l'intérieur de l'Afrique Occidentale*, pp. 206–7.
     (In describing Cabou (Kabu), he gives an account of the origin of the *gelowar*, which he considers were Wolof.)

Hewett, J. F. N.
1857   " On the Jolloffs of West Africa." *R. Geog. Soc. Proc.*, vol. I, pp. 513–17.

Holas, B.
1949   " La clef des songes des mûsulmans sénégalais." *Notes Africaines*, avril, pp. 45–9.
     (Deals with interpretation of dreams.)

Hovelacque, A.
1889   *Les Nègres de l'Afrique Sus-Équatoriale*, pp. 1–28. See also index.

Huntley, Sir Henry
1850   *Seven Years' Service on the Slave Coast of Western Africa*, vol. II. *Twelve months on the Gambia*, pp. 95, 142.

Huxley, E.
1954   *Four Guineas. A Journey through West Africa*, chap. I, pp. 6–7 (Bathurst).
     (A book full of inaccuracies.)

Ingrams, H.
1949   *Seven Across the Sahara*, p. 122.
     (Mentions that Wolof had contributed to the population of Mauritius.)

BIBLIOGRAPHIES

Jectson, Seth
1952   " Njuli Boys : Circumcision rites in the Gambia."   *West African Review*, Oct., p. 1035. (Circumcision at Bathurst.)

Jobson, R.
1932   *The Golden Trade or a discovery of the River Gambra, and the Golden Trade of the Aethiopians* (1620–21). Penguin Press, pp. 65, 80, 108.

Joire, J.
1943   " Archaeological discoveries in Senegal." *Man*, May-June, vol. XLIII, No. 34.
1947   " Amas de coquillages du littoral sénégalais dans la banlieue de Saint-Louis." *Bull. IFAN.*, pp. 170–340.
1951   " La place des Wolofs dans l'Ethnologie Sénégalaise." *Première conférence internationale des Africanistes de l'Ouest. Comptes rendus.* T. II, 'Dakar, pp. 272–3.
1955   " Découvertes archaéologiques dans la région de Rao (Bas-Sénégal), pp. 249–333. *Bull. IFAN.*, T. XVII, juill-oct., pp. 249–333.
     (Pp. 250–95 contain a description of the excavations of tumuli near Rao, which he considers might have been constructed in the 14th century ; pp. 295–329, a survey of traditions and documentary material relating to the period before the 16th century.)

Kane, E. R.
1945   " La disposition des cases des femmes dans le carré du mari commun (Sénégal)." *Notes Africaines*, avr., pp. 11, 14.

Kersaint-Gilly, F. de
1920   " Les Guelowars : leur origine, d'après une légende, très en faveur dans le Saloum oriental." *Bull. du Com. d'Études Hist. et Scient. de l'A.O.F.*, pp. 99–101.

Kilham—see Biller

Labat, J.-B.
1728   *Nouvelle Relation de l'Afrique Occidentale*, 5. vols.

Labouret, H.
1934   In *Les Pêcheurs de Guet N'Dar.*
     (Pp. 295–9 for a description of secret languages in Wolof.)
1941   *Paysans d'Afrique Occidentale.*
     (Methods of apportioning land, pp. 69–71 ; descriptions of political organization in Jolof, pp. 86–90 ; details of taxation, etc., pp. 92–4; caste system, p. 126 ; joking relationship, pp. 140–4.)

Lafont, F.
1938   " Le Gandoul et les Niominkas." *Bull. du Com d'Études Hist. et Scient.*, T. XXI, No. 3, pp. 385–458.
     (Serer, but useful for comparative purposes.)

Lasnet, Dr.
1900   *Une Mission au Sénégal*, pp. 5–6 and 110–35.
     (A general description of the Wolof.)

Leca, N.
1934   *Les Pêcheurs de Guet N'Dar. Bull. du Com. d'Études Hist. et Scient. de l'A.O.F.*, avr-juin, T. XVII, No. 2.

Le Maire,
1682   *Voyage to the Canaries, Cape Verd, and the Coast of Africa under the command of*
(1887)   *M. Dancourt, 1682.* English translation by Edmund Goldsmid, 1887. Privately printed, Edinburgh.

Lemmet, J.
1918   " Contribution à l'étude agrologique de la vallée du Bas-Sénégal." *Bull. du Com. d'Études Hist. et Scient.*, No. 1, jan-mars., pp. 17–56.
     (A description of the regions of the Lac de Guiers and of Taouey.)

Le Mire, P.
1946   " Petite Chronique du Djilor." *Bull. IFAN.*, pp. 55–63.
     (A history of Djilor and Salum.)

Lindsay, J.
1759   *A voyage to the Coast of Africa in 1758.*
     (An account of the expedition to and the capture of the island of Gorée. Little in the way of ethnographic data.)

Macbrair, Rev. R. M.
1861   *The Africans at Home—being a popular description of Africa and the Africans, etc.*, pp. 4–6.

Marche, A.
1879   *Trois Voyages dans l'Afrique Occidentale.* (Description of " griots " (gewεl) pp. 16–17.)

Marmol, Luis del Caravajal
(1520–99) *L'Afrique de Marmol, de la traduction de Nicolas Perrot sieur d'Ablancourt.* Paris, 1667.

THE WOLOF OF SENEGAMBIA

Marty, P.
1933-39 "Islam in French Guinea." *Sierra Leone Studies.* Part I, Dec. 1933; Part II, Dec. 1936; Part III, Jan. 1938; Part IV, Sept. 1939.
(An enormous amount has been published by Marty on Islam in West Africa. Details will be found in the bibliography to Gouilly's *L'Islam dans l'A.O.F.*)

Massé, L.
1954 "Contribution à l'étude de la nuptialité et de la fertilité dans l'agglomération dakaroise." In *Études Sénégalaises*, No. 5.
1956 "Contribution a l'étude de la ville de Thiès—Premier dépouillement numérique sur la situation matrimoniale." *Bull. IFAN.*, pp. 255-80.
(Contains details of marital status, number of wives, etc., pp. 270-3.)

Mauny, R.
1955 "Baobabs—cimetières à griots." *Notes Africaines, IFAN.*, juil, pp. 72-6.

Meeker, O.
1955 *Report on Africa*, pp. 10-11.

Mercier, P.
1954 "Aspects de la société africaine dans l'agglomération dakaroise : groupes familiaux et unités de voisinage." *Études Sénégalaises*, No. 5.
(An outline of results obtained in various sociological investigations in Dakar.)

Mersadier, Y.
1955 "Structure de budgets familiaux à Thiès." *Bull. IFAN.*, T. XVII, No. 3-4, pp. 388-432.
(Analysis of a small sample of budgets in the urban centre of Thiès, the majority of which are Wolof.)

Mills, Lady Dorothy
1929 *The Golden Land*, p. 182.
(A book by a tourist.)

Mitchinson, A. W.
1881 *The Expiring Continent. A narrative of travel in Senegambia . . .*, p. 393.

Moister, W.
1866 *Memorials of Missionary Labours in Western Africa, etc. . . .*, p. 23.

Mollien, G.
1820 *Travels in the interior of Africa to the sources of the Senegal and Gambia . . . in the year 1818.* Ed., Bowdich.

Moloney, Sir A.
1889 "On the melodies of the Volof, Mandingo, Ewe, Yoruba, and Houssa people of West Africa." *Jour. of the Manchester Geog. Soc.*, vol. 5, pp. 277-98.
(Contains only three minute fragments of Wolof music.)

Monod, Th.
1951 *Description de la Côte Occidentale d'Afrique (Sénégal au Cap de Monte, Archipels) par Valentim Fernandes (1506-10).*

Moore, Francis
1730-35 *Travels into the Inland Parts of Africa*, pp. v, vi, 21, 44-6, 51, 61, 71-2, 74, 151-3.

Morgan, Rev. J.
1864 *Reminiscences of the founding of a Christian Mission on the Gambia*, pp. 9-10, 49, 71, 74.

N'Doye, M. C.
1947 (1) "Le boeuf sacré de Diakaho (Sine-Saloum)." *Notes Africaines*, jan., pp. 1-2.
(Ritual sacrifice of a bull to secure a good rainy season and harvest. Serer of Sine-Saloum.)
1947 (2) "La mort d'un bour dans le Saloum." *Notes Africaines*, avr., p. 27.
1948 (1) "Le son du tabala dans le Rip." *Notes Africaines*, avr. pp. 9-10.
(Describes drums with magical properties.)
1948 (2) "La circoncision chez les Sérères-Sine." *Notes Africaines*, avr. p. 21.

Nicolas, F.-J.
1955 "À propos de l'iler." *Notes Africaines*, 66, avr., p. 38.
(Notes similarity between the Wolof hoe and that used in Kordofan.)

Pales, Léon
1952 *Raciologie comparative des Populations de l'A.O.F.*, IV. *Parallèle anatomique succinct des Maures de l'A.O.F., notamment des Maures du Trarza avec des Peuls et des Ouolof.* (Mission Anthropologique de l'A.O.F., 1952.)
1954 *L'Alimentation en A.O.F.*

Papy, L.
1951 "La vallée du Sénégal—Agriculture traditionnelle et riziculture mécanisée." *Cahiers d'Outre Mer.*, No. 16, oct.-déc., and *Études Sénégalaises*, No. 2, *IFAN.*

Park, Mungo
1799 *Travels in the Interior Districts of Africa*, pp. 17, 341-2.
(Contains description of the war between the *Damel* of Kayor and the ruler of Futa Toro.)

BIBLIOGRAPHIES

Parker, H.
1923 " Stone circles in Gambia." *JRAI.*, pp. 173–228.
(Besides the archaeological account, he describes the attitudes of the Wolof towards these remains, and the rites performed to ensure the benevolence of the spirits believed to dwell there.)

Pelissier, P.
1951 " L'arachide au Sénégal—rationalisation et modernisation de sa culture." *Cahiers d'Outre Mer.*, No. 15, juil.-sept., and *Études Sénégalaises*, No. 2, *IFAN.*
(Mentions changes due to the influence of the " Mourides.")

Pommegorge, Pruneau de
1789 *Description de la Nigritie*, pp. 1–10 and 25–50.

Rankin, F. Harrison
1836 *The White Man's Grave. A visit to Sierra Leone in* 1834, vol. I, pp. 227–9.

Reade, W. Winwood
1864 *Savage Africa*, pp. 446–7, 455–7.

Reeve, H. F.
1912 *The Gambia*, pp. 20, 174, 180–8.

R. G. V.—*see* Geoffroy de Villeneuve

Richard-Molard, J.
1949 " Groupes ethniques en A.O.F." In *L'encyclopédie Coloniale et Maritime—Afrique Occidentale Française*, p. 114.
1952 *Afrique Occidentale Française*, pp. 101–2.

R.-M. and J. R.-M.
1950 " Iler ou Hilaire ? " *Notes Africaines*, jan., p. 20.

Robin, J.
1945 " Fondation de Dagana." *Notes Africaines*, jan., p. 3.
1945 " Un exemple d'evolution de l'Afrique rurale. Le rôle progressif des fraternités d'âge sur les rives du Sénégal. " *Farm and Forest.* April–June. Vol. VI. No. 2.
1946 " D'un royaume amphibie et fort disparate. Essai sur l'ancien royaume Sénégalais du Walo." *African Studies*, vol. 5, No. 4, Dec., pp. 250–6.
(A History of Walo.)
1947 " L'évolution du mariage coutumier chez les Musulmans du Sénégal." *Africa*, vol. XVII, July, pp. 192–201.

Roger, Baron
1828 *Fables Sénégalaises, recueillies de l'Ouolof et mises en vers français*, etc.
1829 *Recherches philosophiques sur la langue ouolofe. . . .*

Rousseau, R.
1929 *Le Sénégal d'autrefois. Étude sur le Oualo. Cahiers de Yoro Dyao. Bull. du Com. d'Études Hist. et Scient. de l'A.O.F.*, jan.-juin., T. XII 1–2, pp. 133–211.
1931 *Étude sur le Toubé. Papiers de Rawane Boy*, juil.-sept., T. XIV, No. 3, pp. 334–64.
1933 *Étude sur le Cayor*, avr.-juin., T. XVI, No. 2, pp. 237–98.
1933 " Le village ouolof (Sénégal)." *Annales de Géographie*, XLII, pp. 88–94.
(A good description of Wolof settlements.)
1941–2 " Le Sénégal d'autrefois. Seconde Étude sur le Cayor." *Bull. IFAN.*, pp. 79–144.

Sabatié, A.
n.d. *Le Sénégal, sa conquête et son organisation* (1364–1925), (undated—probably 1926).

Sadji, A.
1954 *Nini. Présence Africaine* 16.
(A novel in French describing life in former days in Saint-Louis.)
See also under Senghor.

Sarr, A.
1949 " Histoire du Sine-Saloum." *Présence Africaine*, 5, pp. 832–7.
(Deals with legendary origin of the *gelowar* and their migrations.)

Saugnier, M.
1791 *Relations de plusieurs voyages à la côte d'Afrique, à Maroc, au Sénégal, à Gorée, à Galam,* etc., pp. 179, 189, 263, 268, 327, 328.
(Describes slave trading.)

Savonnet, G.
1955 (1) " Les villages de la banlieu thièssoise." *Bull. IFAN.*, T. XVII, No. 3–4, pp. 371–87.
(A study of the effects of an urban centre on surrounding villages, two of which are Wolof settlements.)
1955 (2) *La ville de Thiès. Étude de Géographie Urbaine. IFAN.*
(A description of the history, housing, demography, commerce, and industry—the railway workshops—in Thiès ; pp. 158–60 describe the relationship between the caste system and positions held in industry.)

THE WOLOF OF SENEGAMBIA

Schweeger-Hefel, Annemarie
1954 "Einige Bemerkungen zu Wolof-Schmucksachen." *Archiv fur Völkerkunde*. IX. pp. 95–102. (A description of Wolof jewellery.)
Select Committee on West Coast of Africa, 1842, paras. 5692 ; 8007–13 ; 9947, 9968.
Senghor, L., and Sadji, A.
1953 *La belle histoire de Leuk le lièvre*.
(A school reading book in French based on Wolof tales.)
Shoberl, F.
The World in Miniature. Africa. A description of the manners and customs of the Moors of the Zahara, and of the Negro nations between the rivers Senegal and Gambia, 4 vols. Early 19th century.
(A summary which is virtually translated from R. G. V.)
Socé, Ousmane
1942 *Contes et Légendes d'Afrique noire*, Dakar.
(Contains three Wolof stories : pp. 35–8, 45–51, 53–9.)
Suret-Canale, J.
1948 "Quelques aspects de la géographie agraire au Sénégal. Le Cercle de Louga." *Les Cahiers d'Outre-mer.*, oct.-déc., pp. 348–67.
(A very good paper on the agricultural position in a Wolof area.)
Tautain, L.
1885 "Études critiques sur l'ethnologie et ethnographie des peuples du basin du Sénégal." *Revue d'Ethnographie*, IV, pp. 63–8.
Thiam, A. G.
1952 "La circoncision chez les Ouolof." *Notes Africaines*, avr., pp. 49–50.
Thiam, Bodiel
1949 (1) "Hiérarchie de la société ouolove." *Notes Africaines*, jan., p. 12.
1949 (2) "Quelques superstitions ouoloves." *Notes Africaines*, jan., p. 13.
1950 "Coloration des bijoux ouolofs en or de basse qualité." *Notes Africaines*, avr., p. 45.
1954 "Le teugue ou bijoutier ouolof." *Notes Africaines*, jan., pp. 22–5.
Thiam, N'diaga
1949 "L'apprentissage du bijoutier wolof." *Notes Africaines*, avr., p. 53.
de Tressan, M. de L.
1953 "Inventaire linguistique de l'Afrique Occidentale Française et du Togo." *Mém. IFAN.*, No. 30, pp. 146–50.
Geoffroy de Villeneuve (R. G. V.)
1814 *L'Afrique, ou histoire, moeurs, usages et coutumes des Africains*.
Villiers, A., and Leye, Th.
1946 "Le margouillat et la gueule tapée." *Notes Africaines*, oct. p. 23.
(A Wolof story.)
Walckenaer, C. A.
1842 *Collection des Relations de Voyages . . . etc.*, 21 vols.
(A good French source for the writings of early travellers. See especially vols. 2–7 and 12.)
Wills, C.
1951 *White Traveller in Black Africa*, pp. 176–7.
Wilson, J. L.
1856 *Western Africa : its History, Condition and Prospects*, pp. 71–4.

A NOTE ON THE LEBU

In studying the documentary material on the Wolof, one has to extract fragments of information from innumerable books and articles, and there is relatively little modern material. For the Lebu the position is different. They only became a separate entity after their revolt from Kayor, between 1790 and 1810, and in the writings of earlier authors the inhabitants of the Cap Vert Peninsula are not distinguished from those inland. Most of the descriptions of the Lebu as such have been prepared in recent years.

DISTRIBUTION AND POPULATION FIGURES

The Lebu are a fishing people who occupy the coastal zone—Cap Vert Peninsula, Rufisque, and Bargny. In 1949 they numbered 36,000 (16,000 at Dakar, 18,000 at Rufisque, and 2,000 or so in surrounding villages).

LANGUAGE

They speak a dialect of Wolof which differs from that of Jolof and Kayor. A few notes on the dialect are given by Angrand.

ORIGINS

Some consider the Lebu to be a mixture of Wolof from Kayor and Walo with Serer. There are traditions, however, that the first Lebu came from Futa Toro by a slow migration via Jolof, where they were a turbulent element, and from which they had to flee to Kayor after an unsuccessful rebellion. At first many occupied the Dakar peninsula only in the fishing season, returning inland to farm. Other inhabitants may have been fishermen coming from the mouth of the Senegal, an annual movement taking place, the fishermen coming south in November–December driven by the north winds, and waiting for the south-west winds in May–June before returning. The names of the Lebu would seem to indicate that Wolof, Serer, and people from Futa Toro (though whether pre-Fulbe invasion or not is difficult to say), entered into the composition of the population.

HISTORY

At the beginning of the 19th century the Lebu achieved their independence from Kayor under Dial Diop, their struggles lasting from about 1790 to 1812. Fortifications (*tata*) were built across the peninsula, owing their efficacy, according to Corry, as much to their ritual significance as to practical considerations. The peninsula tended to become a refuge for those fleeing from other states. In the 19th century the French, who had occupied the island of Gorée, gained a foothold on the mainland, taking effective possession in 1857, and building the port of Dakar.

PHYSICAL TYPE

In physical type the Lebu are intermediate between the Serer and Wolof. Verneau, however, quoted by Balandier,[1] regards them as the result of a cross between Wolof and Mandinka.

CHARACTER

Angrand [2] describes the character of the Lebu as follows : " le peuple lébou bénéficie de la sagesse des Ouolofs, de la finesse de langage et de l'astuce des Cayoriens, de la roublardise des Baol-Baol, de la sobriété et de l'indifférence des Sérères, joints à un amour inné de la terre. . . . En effet, l'indifférence qu'il manifeste pour tout ce

[1] 1952, p. 8.
[2] 1946, p. 42–3.

93

94   THE WOLOF OF SENEGAMBIA

qui ne le touche pas directement est ce qui caractérise le mieux le Lébou. La diversité d'origines fait de lui un individualiste, un apathique, voire même un timide. . . Les Lébous sont connus pour leur âpreté au gain, et leur astuce . . . economes et avares, ils vivent tous sur le même pied. Jadis aucune manifestation extérieure de richesse ou d'aisance n'était tolérée . . . ''

ECONOMIC LIFE

In contrast to the Serer and Wolof who are above all farmers, the Lebu are fishermen, though millet, rice, and groundnuts are cultivated during the rainy season. Those in the neighbourhood of Dakar go in for market gardening in the fertile hollows. Cassava, of which large amounts are sold in the city, is grown in hedged fields. A few, though this is now mainly an old woman's occupation, make a livelihood from the manufacture of salt by evaporation. There is very little livestock.

Line fishing is carried out in the ocean, fishing with harpoons and seine nets in the bay. Cast nets are used in shallow waters. The canoes have been influenced in form by those from Guet N'Dar, and are more elaborate than the usual dug-out canoes, having wash strakes added, and points fore and aft projecting out of the water. Sails of a type borrowed from Europe have long been in use. Outboard motors are now being adopted. Some fish is sold fresh ; any surplus to market requirements is split open and dried in the sun. The work of preparing and selling fish is mainly in the hands of the women.

SOCIAL AND POLITICAL ORGANIZATION

Like the Wolof, the Lebu live in compounds of square thatched huts. The system of government evolved by the Lebu after their independence was as follows : the heads of compounds formed a ward council under a president (bɔrɔm pinch), which delegated two or three members to the village council, or to that called the Njambur Ndakaru which regulated the affairs of the collectivity. The njambur elected the Seriny Ndakaru, who was originally both a religious chief and a war leader. The seriny were elected from the families of Diop or Diol. After election the seriny was isolated for eight days and had to undergo certain rites. In the work of government he was controlled and assisted by the ndei ji reu the representative of the people, and the ndei njambur the representative of the nobles, but he himself appointed the jaraf who looked after the finances and land questions, and the saltigi who acted as leader in war, and in times of peace saw that the seriny's orders were carried out. The seriny also nominated the Imam of the mosque who acted as supreme judge. The young men had representatives (Fereny Ndakaru) who acted as intermediaries between them and the seriny, and organized collective labour when required.

The young people, both boys and girls, were organized in age-sets (mas or mes). That of the girls broke up on the marriage of its members, that of the boys continued into adult life, and might be used as the basis of co-operation in fishing activities.

Emphasis on matrilineal descent remained stronger than among the Wolof. The authority of the father was weak, compared with the mother's brother, with whom a young man often lived. Certain property, the rights to lands and over herds, remained in the hands of the eldest male of the matrilineage, who had the rights of usufruct, and he could not dispose of them without the consent of his potential heirs. Personal property could be transmitted in the male line, though when it was shared one-third was paid to the maternal line (sometimes going to the nephews, sometimes the mother's brother) two-thirds to the children.

RELIGION

Though the original head of the Lebu collectivity was a Muslim, and Islamic law was adopted as the basis of the Lebu constitution, animism continued to flourish among the people, and widespread conversion to Islam is fairly recent. Most Lebu

A NOTE ON THE LEBU

belong to the Tijaniya ; a few are Mourides, while some belong to the Layen, a sect peculiar to the Lebu. The teachings peculiar to this sect are [3] : that the pilgrimage to Mecca is not necessary (a manifestation of the Lebu desire for independence) ; that the number of wives a man may have is not limited; and an insistence on cleanliness both of body and of housing. Women are admitted into the mosque, though they are separated from the men (an indication of the important role of Lebu women in society).

Pagan cults are at present maintained by the women. On the peninsula are the abodes (trees, lakes, rocks, etc.) of various spirits, of the land, of villages, of the sea, to whom offerings of sour milk, millet, etc., are made to ensure peace and freedom from trouble. Ritual dances are performed to bring rain and cure certain diseases. Each family group also has its own spirits, often believed to reside in a large jar, filled with water and various roots and looked after by a woman. It is to her that people go for invocations, divinations, etc. Ritual sacrifices of millet, sour milk, etc., are made and, on very serious occasions, an animal.

Possession of spirits, followed by dances of exorcism, sacrifice and the creation of personal altars to the spirit, are still common among the women.

With neighbouring peoples, they share beliefs in the evil eye, the devil, bad spirits, witches, and so on.

CHANGES IN LEBU SOCIETY [4]

The growth of Dakar (population in 1932, 61,400 ; 1942, 102,000 ; 1947, 175,000; 1953, about 260,000), now the third largest port of the French Union, a centre for international airlines, a railway terminus, and the seat of government of A.O.F., has tended to swamp the Lebu. The old settlements in the urban zone of Dakar have been displaced, and the outlying villages now find themselves in the midst of residential quarters, industrial enterprises, and military installations. They still retain something of their identities as villages by maintaining a high degree of self-sufficiency, the land and sea still furnishing their traditional resources, and the city providing a market for both fish and garden produce.

The population of the Lebu villages (Ouakam, Yoff, N'Gor, Tiaroye, Cambérène) doubled in eight years, due both to the excess of births over deaths and to the influx of strangers, especially Tukulors, Fulbe, Mauretanians, Bambara, Jola, and to a lesser extent Serer, Susu, and Wolof.

With the vast modern building programme and the growth of industrial plants, many young men have abandoned their traditional occupations and become labourers (especially stone breakers in the quarries) and masons, or are employed in industry, while a few are to be found in commerce and transport. Some are labourers only in the dry season, farming in the rains. A tendency has been noted for the young men, when space is cramped in their compounds, to split off and form separate compounds of their own. Whereas among the older generation of farmers polygyny was usual, monogamy is commoner among labourers—the younger men.

The degree of urbanization varies according to distance from the city. Certain villages (Kamba, Cambérène) remain villages with their traditional economy of fishing and agriculture. Hann, on the other hand, is almost entirely urbanized. Ouakam and Yoff show a marked tendency to urbanization. Permanent houses are often built, and houses, especially those of traders and craftsmen, are built along the roads. The growth in the number of traders indicates an increased standard of living. Tiaroye-gare has grown up near the railway line.

---

[3] Balandier, 1952, p. 110.
[4] Based largely on Gallais, 1954.

BIBLIOGRAPHY

Angrand, A.-P.
1943   *Manuel Français-Ouolof.*
        (Notes on Lebu dialect, pp. 90–93.)
1946 ?   *Les Lébous de la Presqu'île du Cap-Vert.* Dakar.
Badiane, D. M.
1947   " Les faire-part de mariage Lébou et les réponses." *Notes Africaines*, No. 36, p. 30.
Balandier, G.
1946 (1) " Observations sur le patrimoine, et l'héritage chez les Lébou de Bargny." *Notes Africaines*, No. 32, pp. 18–9.
1946 (2) " Notes sur l'exploitation du sel par les vieilles femmes de Bargny." *Notes Africaines*, No. 32, p. 22.
1948 (1) " Femmes ' possédées ' et leurs chants." *Présence Africaine*, No. 5, pp. 749–54.
1948 (2) " L'enfant chez les Lébou du Sénégal." *Enfance*, No. 4, sept.-oct., pp. 285–304.
Balandier, G., and Mercier, P.
1952   *Les Pêcheurs Lébou.*
        (Deals especially with education, religion and magic, and fishing techniques.)
Balandier, G., and Holas, B.
1946   " Quelques ' Galat ' de pêche observés à M'Bao." *Notes Africaines*, No. 32, oct., p. 20.
        (Describes charms used on canoes, nets, etc., to obtain good fishing, protection against danger and damage to nets, etc.)
Corry, J.
1807   *Observations upon the Windward Coast of Africa.*
        (Pp. 10–17 describes a visit to Gorée and Dakar.)
Duchemin, M. G.-J.
1949   " La république Lébou et le peuplement actuel " in " La Presqu'île du Cap-Vert." *Études Sénégalaises, IFAN.*, pp. 289–304.
Gallais, J.
1954   " Les villages lébous de la Presqu'île du Cap Vert." *Cahiers d'Outre Mer*, 26, avr.-juin.
        (A good account of changes in the types of settlement, economy, etc., in the neighbourhood of Dakar.)
Gouilly, A.
1952   *L'Islam dans l'Afrique Occidentale Française.*
        (Pp. 167–8 describes the Layen sect.)
Holas, B.
1948   " Moyens de protection magique chez les Lébou." *Notes Africaines*, No. 39, pp. 19–24.
        (Detailed description of charms and amulets and their purposes.)
Leca, N.
1934   *Les Pêcheurs de Guet N'Dar.*
        (Contains useful descriptions of canoe construction, types of nets, identification of fishes, fishing techniques, etc.)
Mauny, R.
1943   " Les murs tatas de Dakar." *Notes Africaines*, No. 17, pp. 1–2.
1948   " Du nouveau sur les murs tata de Dakar." *Notes Africaines*, No. 40, pp. 14–15.
        (Draws attention to Corry's remarks on the *tata*.)
Michel, C.
1934   " L'organisation coutumière (sociale et politique) de la collectivité Léboue de Dakar." *Bull. Com. d' Ét. Hist. et Scient. de l'A.O.F.*, T. XVII, No. 3, pp. 510–24.
        (Description of the old political organization of the Lebu.)
Mercier, P.
1946   " Un épervier utilisé par un pêcheur de petit M'Bao." *Notes Africaines*, No. 32, p. 11.
        (Description of the cast net.)
Sylla, Assane
1955   " Une République Africaine au XIXe siècle (1795–1857)." *Présence Africaine*, avr.-juil., pp. 47–65.
        (History of the Lebu and an account of the French occupation of the Dakar peninsula.)

A NOTE ON THE SERER[1]

INTRODUCTION

The Serer now occupy an area marginal to the Wolof. They clearly represent an " older " element in the population of this area, though Serer (or people like them) may have entered into the composition of the Wolof as an ethnic entity. From the 16th century onwards they were subject to raids by Wolof chiefs, and much of the Serer area was gradually incorporated in the Wolof political system. A Wolof ruling class took over the government, and though some of the Serer leading families may have become " Wolof," the majority of the incorporated Serer occupied a low peasant status. The states of Sine and Salum achieved varying degrees of independence at different times, and in areas difficult of access pockets of Serer remained independent of Wolof chiefs until modern times. Many people of Serer origin now speak Wolof rather than Serer, while Serer speech has taken over many Wolof words. Consequently, in Sine-Salum in particular, one often cannot determine whether particular traits should be regarded as Wolof or Serer.

NOMENCLATURE

The Serer are known to the Wolof as *Serer* ; to the Fulbe as *Sererab'e* (sing. *Serer*). In old literature they appear as Sereos (Fernandes, 1506) ; Cereres (Labat, 1728) ; Serera (Adanson, 1749) ; Cereses and Serays (Durand, 1806) ; Serreres (Mollien, 1818).

DISTRIBUTION

The Serer occupy roughly the zone south of the railway between Thiès and Kaffrine, and reaching south almost to the Gambia. (See end map.) De Tressan (1953, p. 150) gives the following detailed distribution : " la partie sud du cercle de Diourbel, la subdivision de Mbour, la partie sud de la subdivision de Guinguine, la subdivision de Kaolack, en tiers avec Wolof et Bambara, la subdivision de Fatick, la partie Nord de la subdivision de Foundiougne ; ils constituent des îlots dans la subdivision de Tivaouane, celles de Thiès et Nioro du Rip. Leur habitat est donc en gros le Sine et une partie du Baol et du Saloum."

DEMOGRAPHY

Population

Source	Year	Estimate of total Serer population
Lasnet 1900	1900	180,000
Le Gouvernement général de l'A.O.F. 1926	1926	229,387
L'encyclopédie coloniale et maritime 1949	1949	265,000
de Tressan 1950	1950	306,468

(The figure for 1950 includes various regional sub-groups, 3,500 Ndut,[2] about 5,000 Non, and about 9,000 Nyominka.)

In the Gambia the Serer number between two and four thousand.

Density

The density of population in the Serer zone is higher than in most of the Senegal, being over 50 per square kilometre (130 per square mile) south of the Thiès-Guinguineo railway line, 35–50 in the coastal belt, and 20–35 in Salum.

---

[1] This summary of the Serer is based on the literature quoted in the bibliography. My acquaintance with the Serer is limited to sporadic contacts with those found in fishing settlements in the Gambia.

[2] See below, p. 99.

THE WOLOF OF SENEGAMBIA

Vital Statistics

The following data based on Mission records are given by Brasseur for the Christian community of Mont-Roland (Serer Ndut). The ratio of men to women was 109/100 ; marriage rate 8·5 per 1,000 ; age of marriage for men 21–24, for women 18–20 ; birthrate 45 per 1,000. An average of five children (not counting stillbirths or deaths before baptism) were born per family. Of the children 26% died before the end of the first year, 44% before three years.

HOUSES AND SETTLEMENTS

In the 19th century the Serer occupied compact isolated villages, generally surrounded by a clearing, but with forest nearby where people and animals could, if necessary, take refuge. With the establishment of peace there has been a tendency for villages to be more dispersed and smaller in size. The siting of the villages of the Nyominka of the coastal region is largely determined by the availability of fresh water.

Lafont gives the population of the Nyominka region of Gandoul in 1937 as 4,051 in 289 compounds (average size 14) and 11 villages (average 368).

Houses are either square or round, made of reeds and millet stalks, and thatched with grass. Brasseur describes rectangular houses built at Fadiout from blocks of " chalk " (made from oyster shells), shell, and sand. Serer living near creeks generally build their storehouses on piles raised out of the water.

PHYSICAL CHARACTERISTICS

The Serer are fairly tall (172 cm.), almost as dark as the Wolof, but usually not so fine-featured, nostrils being broader and lips more everted. In fishing communities especially, the men are of an athletic build, extremely strong, with well-developed muscles and broad shoulders.

GROUPING

Most of the earlier writers have divided the Serer into two groups, the Serer-Non, who occupy the basin of the Tamna, and the Serer-Sine, who occupy Sine-Salum.

Some sources (e.g., *Gambia Annual Report* for 1885) distinguish the Nyominka from the Serer. In modern Gambian tribal statistics they are grouped together. The Nyominka can be considered as a sub-group of the Serer inhabiting the coastal region and specializing in fishing, while the majority of the Serer live inland and are farmers. A classification of the Serer based on linguistic affiliations is given on p. 99.

TRIBAL INTERMIXTURE

The traditions of the Serer (see below) would seem to indicate mixture with Fulbe, Mandinka, Jola, Bainunka, and other peoples. In the present century their country has been further penetrated by Wolof, and by Sudanese groundnut farmers (Bambara, Serahuli, etc.). Intermarriage between Serer and other tribes was formerly punished by banishment.

TRADITIONS OF ORIGIN, EARLY MOVEMENTS AND INTER-TRIBAL RELATIONSHIPS

Fulbe and Serer : Boilat (1853, p. 389) quotes a tradition that when the Fulbe, under pressure from the Mauretanians, took refuge on the banks of the Senegal (i.e., Futa Toro), they found a primitive people there (i.e., the Serer) who were driven out into Kayor and Baol. .A second version states that when the Fulbe arrived in Futa Toro, they were received as friends by the Serer, who were pagans like themselves, and that they lived together in peace and intermarried, becoming the Tukulor. Tautain (1885, p. 68) states that the Tukulor claimed that the Serer were their former slaves who had escaped.

Jola and Serer : A Jola tradition, quoted among others by Wintz (1909, pp. v–vi), gives the Jola and Serer a common origin in Kabu (Haute Gambie and Portuguese Guinea) from which, because of internal quarrels, and probably also because of Mandinka and Fulbe pressure, emigration took place under two sisters, one (Anécho) establishing herself in the basin of the Salum and becoming the " mother " of the Serer, the other (Aguène) going to Casamance and becoming the " mother " of the Jola. A joking relationship exists between Jola and Serer to this day.

Mandinka and Serer : According to Ezanno (1919) the Serer of Fadiout came from Kabu under a Mandinka chief, Mansa Ali. Gambian traditions would seem to indicate that the original inhabitants of Nyomi were Serer, subject to the Wolof chiefs of Salum. They called in Mandinka and Fulbe warrior chiefs to help them in their struggle for independence. These took over the chieftainship of Nyomi, and in the course of time the country became Mandinka.

During the religious wars of the last century the people of the coastal region were attacked by the Mandinka and many were converted to Islam.

Serer and Bainunka : Bérenger-Féraud (1879) considers that the Bainunka also entered into the composition of the Serer.

These traditions all suggest that the Serer represent the survivors of a primitive people who migrated westwards to the coast from various starting points under Wolof, Mandinka, and Fulbe pressure, and were later dominated by these.

LANGUAGE

Serer is classified by Westermann and Bryan (1952) as a Larger Unit of the West Atlantic Languages. Earlier writers (Bérenger-Féraud, Faidherbe, Cust, etc.) divided the Serer language into two, Serer-Kégèm (Kéguem) or Ndyégèm (Ndjeguem), and Serer-Non (None), the latter subdivided into None, Faros, and Safi. De Tressan (1953, para. 534) classifies the numerous dialects as " true " and " false."

The group of " true " dialects includes :—

Sinsin (wrongly called Ndyégèm or Kégèm by Delafosse and Homburger), spoken in Sine.

Ndyégèm, the name of a group of six villages north of Ngasobil (Ndiémane, Ndolor, Sandiaye, Diokar, Oungoulbine, and Aga).

Baolbaol, spoken in Baol, and which is Sinsin, penetrated lexically by Wolof.

Fadyut-Palmerin (" dialecte de la petite côte "), spoken at Fadiout, south of Joal and at Palmerin Point. This differs phonetically and lexically from Sinsin.

The dialects of the islands of *Nyomi.*

The group of " false " dialects includes :—

Safènsafèn, spoken in the south-west of the canton Diobas (subdivision of Thiès) and in the cantons Mbayard-Nianing and Sandak-Diaganao of the subdivision of Mbour.

Non, at Doga, Saout, in the subdivision of Tivaouane, at Fandème, in the subdivision of Thiès, and in the canton Thor-Ndiendèr, around Thiès.

Ndut, at Pakoumkouye, Pallo, Loukhous, Tivagne-Diassène, Sambay-Maran, Mont-Roland, Foulom, in the subdivision of Tivaouane, as well as at Thiès.

Similarities between Serer-Kégèm and Fula have been pointed out by Greffier (1901), Guiraudon (1894), and Homburger (1939). Homburger regards Serer as an archaic form of Fula. Greenberg (1952) considers the relationship between Serer and Fula as obvious as the relationship between French and Italian. On the other hand de Tressan would not classify Fula and Serer together. It would appear that the relationship cannot be determined on the evidence available. The link lies between Fula and one dialect of Serer, but it is not known how much this Serer dialect resembles or differs from others. It is not even certain that Lamoise's or Greffier's dictionaries (from which most of the comparisons seem to have been made) include words of only one dialect. Furthermore, both the phonetics and grammatical analyses of these

THE WOLOF OF SENEGAMBIA

early students of Serer are, by modern standards, faulty. Finally, it has to be decided with which dialect of Fula (in the absence of " basic Fula ") it should be compared.

All one can justifiably say at present is that a number of extremely common roots (the words for come, hear, know, sleep, hard, wide, far, hot, cold, laugh, fall, chew, follow, white, black, kill, count, ask, bitter, sweet, etc.) are common to both Serer-Kégèm and Fula. The Serer verbal system, however, seems distinct (not having the Fula three-voice system), though a number of verbal infixes are similar. Both have a system of noun classes, but on analysis these have little resemblance. Both languages have a system of consonant alternances (this is a common feature of Senegambian languages), but Serer seems much more irregular, and, according to Homburger, a *w* in Fula might correspond to a *b*, *p*, *k*, *f*, *v*, *g*, or ' in Serer, a *b* in Fula to *mb*, *b*, *f*, *p*, *v*, or ', and a *d* to *t*, *r*, *nd*, *d*, etc., so that she gives as examples, Fula *mau* corresponding to *mak* in Serer, *waw* to *vag*, *haw* to *hup*, *tau* to *ref*, etc.

It would seem that the vocabulary common to the two languages forms in reality a small proportion of the total vocabularies, and many words seem to be concerned with household work and food (eat, drink, be thirsty, be hungry, meat, oil, fish, rice, baobab leaf, pound, cook, light fire, put out fire, spread to dry, clean cotton, dry, cut, dye, well [of water], gourd, etc.), and domestic animals (donkey, cow, sheep, horse)—the type of vocabulary which could be transferred through intermarriage or other association between two neighbouring tribes.

Thus, until reliable analyses of the grammatical systems of the various Serer dialects have been made, the derivation of Serer from Fula, of Fula from Serer, of both from a common source, or determination of the extent of interpenetration, rests on insufficient evidence.

According to Sacleux, in spite of the tradition that the Serer and Jola have a common origin, Serer Sin is totally distinct from Jola. The vocabularies are completely independent, the grammars very divergent, and though there is in both a division of nouns into classes, these are by different procedures. He finds a close resemblance between Jola and a vocabulary of Portuguese Guinea given in Koelle's *Polyglotta* (1854) called Sarar. There is no record of Serer in this region in present-day ethnographic accounts, and it is extremely doubtful whether Sarar has any connection with Serer.

ECONOMY

The Serer have a mixed economy, keeping cattle, growing millet for food (rice as well where conditions are suitable), and cultivating groundnuts as a cash crop. As among the Wolof an early ripening bulrush millet (*pod*) is grown in a continuous belt round the compounds, with small plots of cassava and cotton interspersed. The land farther away is (where soil and demographic conditions permit) divided into three sections, one devoted to groundnuts, one to millet, while the third is manured by the cattle. Hedges reinforced with branches are planted between the zone occupied by the herds and the growing crops, and along cattle paths through cultivated areas. A three-year rotation of pasture fallow, followed by millet, followed by groundnuts, is maintained.

As a result of their farming methods, the vegetation of much of the Serer zone has become parkland characterized by the tree *kad* (Acacia albida), which sheds its leaves before the rains (so not interfering with groundnuts planted in its vicinity, and adding valuable organic matter to the soil just before the planting season) and maintains its leaves in the dry season, thereby providing a valuable source of fodder for cattle at a time when grazing is scarce.

The cash received from groundnuts, after payment of taxes and purchase of clothing, is mainly devoted to building up herds of cattle.

Serer (Nyominka) in the coastal zone find themselves in an environment unsuited for farming and stock raising (though the women work rice fields), and rely on exchanging fish, salt, dried shellfish, etc., for millet from inland peoples. Fish are caught with nets, lines and hooks, spears, and fish traps (in creeks). The fish, if not sold fresh, are split open and dried in the sun, though in the rainy season they may be smoked.

Serer girls before marriage often go as domestic servants to urban centres—Bathurst, Dakar, Thiès, etc. The sellers of *chere* [3] in large markets are frequently Serer women, though Futa Jalon Fulbe women also specialize in this commodity.

Nyominka come from the Senegal to the Gambia during the dry season as fishermen and traders and along the river at the heads of creeks where canoes can be landed are " camps," sometimes with permanent residents, where those sailing on the river can find lodging places.

Political Organization

According to Fernandes (1506–10) the Serer were not yet in his time subject to the king of Canagaa (i.e., the Wolof ruler), and had neither king nor lord. The Wolof had made efforts to conquer them, but had not been successful owing to the difficulties of the terrain. Elsewhere, however, he refers to the Barbacijs (i.e., people of the Bar Sine, *bar* being the Serer equivalent of the wolof *bur*, king) which seems to imply that a higher political order had been established in that area. Part of the Serer zone however, seems to have been more fully incorporated later with the extension of Wolof domination, and the rulers of Kayor did not regard the chiefs of Sine and Salum as being essentially different from themselves. So far as one can judge, indigenous leaders were supplanted by Wolof warrior chiefs often closely related to the *bur*.

But behind the Wolof system of rule, and in areas unconquered by them, one can see an indigenous society with other characteristics—a society without caste groups,[4] with no central political system, where the village head had very restricted powers, where the feud played an important part in relationships between local groups, where law and order were maintained by supernatural sanctions (trial by ordeal, cursing a wrongdoer), and where priests and priestesses of cults played an important part in society.

Social Organization [5]

The Serer are organized in exogamous matrilineages which may be localized or dispersed, and the family group of man, wife, and children is of limited importance. A wife joins her husband's community, and is provided with land to farm and a house. The husband is responsible for feeding his wife, but not for clothing her. Earnings or goods acquired by the wife from her labours continue to go to the head of her matrilineage. A boy stays with his father until circumcision, which may be performed at any time up to the age of about 25. After this he may join his mother's brother. If he continues to stay with his father, he will help him on his farms and be fed in return, but he has the right to inherit only a hut, tools, weapons, and ornaments from his father, and not land. If the father dies before the boy is circumcised, he would stay with his father's brother until circumcision.

Land appears to be held collectively by matrilineages of uncertain span. The plots of a matrilineage holding may be dispersed over a wide area.

The care of matrilineage property (cattle, land, cash, etc.) is vested in its head, who enjoys its use, but cannot dispose of it without the consent of the members of the lineage, and in particular of his successor. He takes over the millet from stores

---

[3] See page 37.

[4] Among the Serer, leatherworkers and smiths, weavers and potters were, and are, generally Mandinka or Wolof. Slavery was not known prior to Wolof penetration (Lasnet, 1900 ; cf. Lafont, 1938).

[5] No detailed study of Serer kinship appears to have been made, and even kinship terminology has not been systematically recorded.

102 THE WOLOF OF SENEGAMBIA

of deceased members of the community, gives consent for marriages and receives marriage-payments and damages paid in respect of a member of the matrilineage ; in return he makes arrangements for funeral ceremonies, pays fines on behalf of members, and in some areas marriage money for young men. The efforts of members are devoted to increasing the heritage of the matrilineage.

In a society with a minimum of personal property, an elaborate code of regulations has been developed governing sales, gifts of property, letting of fields, hiring cattle, hiring garments and ornaments for special occasions, contracts for the services of artisans (weavers, leatherworkers, etc.), and the pledging of property. Dulphy's account should be consulted for detailed descriptions.

Marriage involves the payment of palm-wine and a bar of iron when asking for the girl, a bull and more palm-wine as marriage-payment (though a money payment could be made instead). The consent of the girl's mother's brother is essential, though in some Serer communities the father would also be asked, and would receive a marriage-payment. A woman without relatives would receive the marriage money herself.

A ceremonial seizure of the girl by the bridegroom's relatives and friends, with the bride's matrikin trying to prevent them taking her away, seems to have been common in all Serer groups.

When a girl was made pregnant before a marriage-payment had been made, the children belonged to the mother's group. A woman who was sterile could pay the marriage money for a girl, have her made pregnant and claim the children as her own.

At the present time with the development of the cash crop economy, greater mobility, the influence of Islam and of Catholic Missions, there has been a greater emphasis on individual property.

Funerals [6] are the most important occasions for the gathering of kinsfolk and neighbours. After death the body is washed, then covered with oil or butter, and wrapped in cloths. The women cry, while the men fire guns. The body is put in a grave outside the village, and covered with mats and branches. A roof is put over it, and this is covered with earth from a surrounding ditch, or shells. A man's pipe and tobacco, and some millet and water are put with him. The grave of a man is marked by his bow and arrow, that of a woman by her mortar and pestle. Formerly the bodies of *gewel* were put in baobab trees or exposed on platforms on trees (Valtaud). After a burial the community turns to feasting, dancing, and drinking.

RELIGIOUS BELIEFS AND CULTS

While the Wolof readily adopted Islam,[7] although still retaining many of their pagan beliefs, the Serer showed themselves strongly resistant. During the religious wars of the last century many were massacred or committed suicide rather than be converted. Catholic Missions have worked among the Serer since the middle of last century, but with limited success.

The Serer consider that after death the spirit wanders about for a while near home and is nourished by a tenuous substance, evaporated from the food presented to it. Finally the spirit becomes incorporated in either an animate or inanimate body, a lizard, a snake, or a tree. The fear of provoking the ill-will of spirits leads to the dead being buried with signs of the greatest respect. The spirits are appeased or invoked in ceremonies composed of invocations, palm-wine libations, offerings of millet, and sacrifices of animals.

Describing the beliefs of the Serer of Fadiout, Ezanno (1919) states that the *Tyahanora* (a matriclan ?) were considered lords of the sea. A " king " was chosen, whose function it was to attract fish to the coast, and to make sacrifices to the spirit

---

[6] For burial see particularly Labat, Vol. IV, p. 157 ; Dulphy, p. 232–3 for variations in the type of grave.

[7] See above, p. 70.

A NOTE ON THE SERER

of the sea, which was incarnated in a lizard living in a hollow baobab. The " king " could be deposed if he failed to bring the fish.

The *Pédyor* were considered to own the land and water. " A Pédyor was a cousin of the Creator", and the oldest of the women of this group was in charge of rain-making, and of stopping rain when it was too abundant.

The *Patafata* owned the salt.

The Creator (*Rog*) was considered benevolent, and therefore did not need to be propitiated. It seems however that his help was invoked in case of hostile invasion.[8]

Other spirits (*pangol*) lived in little houses [9] built at the foot of a large cotton or fig tree. Inside such a hut was kept an upturned pot and potsherds, where libations of milk, millet, etc., were made. Priestesses established cults, making known the desires of these spirits, and predicting disasters. In case of illness or death (which was attributed to supernatural causes) recourse would be had to a priestess to find out who (through sorcery) or what spirit (through maliciousness) was responsible.

Special dances were held to bring rain, when the women dressed as men, and with lances, harpoons, and guns made threatening gestures at the sky. A second method was a ceremony called *dun* in which children at nightfall presented their bare backsides to a passing raincloud. A similar action was performed when passing Cape Nase to the spirit *Kumba Tyupan*,[10] who would ruin the voyage unless this were done.

The cult of a spirit, *Tahar*, was widely practised. A Serer could vow his enemy together with his maternal line to this spirit and death would carry them off one by one. All the property of a person killed by *Tahar* came to the head of the cult. Cases of theft and suspected sorcery were also dealt with by its priests. A feast of the dead (*Tyéké*) [11] was celebrated before the beginning of the new agricultural year. Guns were fired, and each man went to sit on the grave of his ancestors. Offerings of rice and millet were made, a taste of brandy was poured on it, while the rest was drunk in honour of the ancestors. Special dances (*pol*) followed. The ceremony also marked the end of the period of mourning for those who became widows during the year.

DRESS AND APPEARANCE

In former days Serer men and women wore only a loincloth, though the women when outside the compound put on a short skirt reaching to the knees; but as a result of contact with the Wolof on the one hand and Catholic missionaries on the other, they have adopted much the same type of dress as the Wolof.

Formerly women had their bodies tattooed at puberty with a metallic point dipped in the juice of the *darkasu* fruit, which resulted in the formation of keloids. Men wore ear-rings, and women and girls had coins and beads on a string attached to their hair, bracelets of copper on their arms, and beads round their neck and waist. Under Wolof domination the Serer were forbidden to wear gold or silver.

---

[8] *Gambia Annual Report*, 1885.

[9] Such a house still exists in the Mandinka village of Jammekunda (Central Baddibu) in the Gambia.

[10] A similar custom was for long performed at a point in the River Gambia for Mama Yunkume. This is described by Stibbs (*Journal of a Voyage up the Gambia*, 1723); Poole (*Life, Scenery and Customs in Sierra Leone and the Gambia*, 1850, II, p. 146); Morgan (1864, pp. 100–1); and Reade (1864, p. 148). For details of the last two titles see Wolof bibliography, pp. 90 and 91 above.

[11] See also p. 71.

104 THE WOLOF OF SENEGAMBIA

LINGUISTIC BIBLIOGRAPHY

Anon. (St. Joseph de Ngasobil)
> 1880 *Guide de la conversation en quatre langues : français, volof, anglais, sérèr.*

Cust, R. N.
> 1883 *A sketch of the modern languages of Africa,* pp. 175–6.

Diop, Cheikh Anta
> 1948 " Études de linguistique ouolove." *Présence Africaine,* 4, pp. 672–84.

Ezanno, F. J.
> 1953 " Quelques proverbes sérèrs recueilles à Fadiout (Sénégal)." *Anthropos,* vol. 48 pp. 593–6.

Faidherbe, Le Général
> 1865 " Étude sur la langue Kéguem ou Sérère-Sine." *Annuaire du Sénégal.*
> 1887 *Langues sénégalaises, Wolof, Arabe-Hassania, Soninké, Sérère, Notions Grammaticales, Vocabulaires et phrases,* pp. 55–72 Grammatical notes ; pp. 171–205 Vocabulary pp. 249–266 Sentences.

Greenberg, J. H.
> 1955 *Studies in African Linguistic classification.*—The classification of Fulani.

Greffier, H.
> 1901 *Dictionnaire français-sérère, précédé d'un abrégé de la grammaire sérère.*

De Guiraudon, T. G.
> 1894 *Bolle Fulbe. Manuel de la langue Foule.*
> (List of words common to Fula and Serer, pp. 133–5.)

Hestermann, F.
> 1915 " Die repetition in der Serersprache von Senegambia." *Zeitschrift des deutschen Morgenländischen Gesellschaft,* LXIX, pp. 107–12.
> " Der dreistufige Anlaut und die Suffixbildung im Serer." *Weiner Zeitschrift für die Kunde des Morgenländes,* XXX, pp. 223–63.

Homburger, L.
> 1939 " Le Sérère-Peul." *Journ. de la Soc. des African.,* T. IX, pp. 85–102.

Lamoise, P.
> 1873 *Dictionnaire de la langue sérère.*
> 1873 *Grammaire de la langue sérère avec des exemples et des exercices.*

Mollien, G.
> 1820 *Travels in the Interior of Africa to the sources of the Senegal and Gambia* (p. 379, short vocabulary of Serer).

Senghor, L. S.
> 1944 " L'harmonie vocalique en sérère (Dialecte du Dyéguème)." *Journ. de la Soc. des African.,* T. XIV, pp. 17–23.

de Tressan, Marquis
> 1953 *Inventaire Linguistique de l'Afrique Occidentale Française et du Togo* Mem. IFAN No. 30. pp. 150–7.

Wintz, Ed.
> 1909 *Dictionnaire Français-Dyola et Dyola- Français.*
> (Introduction pp. v–vi gives tradition of common origin for Serer and Jola ; pp. ix–x, discussion of linguistic position by Ch. Sacleux.)

GENERAL BIBLIOGRAPHY

Adanson, M.
> 1759 *A voyage to Senegal, the Isle of Gorée, and the River Gambia* (1749–53), pp. 158–9, 162, 165.

Aujas, L.
> 1925 " Funérailles royales et ordre de succession au trône chez les Sérères du Sine." *Bull. du Com. d'Études Hist. et Scient.,* T. VIII, No. 3, pp. 501–8.
> 1931 Les Sérères du Sénégal (Moeurs et coutumes de droit privé). *Bull. du Com. d'Études Hist. et. Scient.,* pp. 293–333.

Bérenger-Féraud, L.-J.-B.
> 1879 *Les Peuplades de la Sénégambie,* pp. 273–84.

Boilat, L'Abbé P. D.
> 1853 *Esquisses Sénégalaises,* pp. 389–90. Traditions of Fulbe/Serer contacts.

Bourgeau, J.
> 1933 " Notes sur la coutume des Sérères du Sine et du Saloum." *Bull. du Com. d'Études Hist. et Scient.,* T. XVI, No. 1, pp. 1–65.

Brasseur, G.
> 1950 " Demographie des Ndout." *Notes Africaines,* No. 48, pp. 121–3.
> (Demographic data for the Christian population from Mission records.)
> 1952 " À propos des maisons en dur de Fadiout." *Notes Africaines,* No. 56, pp. 117–9.

BIBLIOGRAPHY

Carlus, J.
1880 "Les Sérères de la Sénégambie." *Revue de Géographie*, VI juin pp. 409–420 ; VII juillet pp. 30–37 ; VII août pp. 98–105.

Corré, A.
1883 " Les Sérères de Joal et de Portudal." *Revue d'Ethnographie*., vol. II, pp. 1–20.

Dulphy, G.
1937 " Coutume des Sérères None (Cercle de Thiès)." In *Coutumiers Juridiques de l'Afrique Occidentale Française* (1939).
1936 " Coutume sérère de la Petite-Côte (Cercle de Thiès)." *Ibid.*, pp. 237–321.

Ezanno, R. P.
1919 " Fadiout (Village Sérère)." *Bull. du Com. d'Études Hist. et Scient.*, No. 1, pp. 68–74.

Fayet, J. C.
1937 "Coutume des Sérères N'Doute (Cercle de Thiès)." In *Coutumiers Juridiques de l'Afrique Occidentale Française* (1939), pp. 195–212.

Fernandes—*see* Monod

Gambia
1885 Annual Report on the Blue Book.

Hovelacque, A.
1889 *Les Nègres de l'Afrique Sus-Equatoriale*, pp. 28–34.

Labat, J.-B.
1728 *Nouvelle relation de l'Afrique Occidentale*, vol. IV, pp. 156–9, 171.

Lafont, F.
1938 " Le Gandoul et les Niominkas." *Bull. du Com. d'Études Hist. et Scient.*, T. XXI, No. 3, pp. 385–458.

Lasnet, Dr.
1900 *Une Mission au Sénégal*, pp. 6–7, 137–50.

Monod, Th.
1951 *Description de la Côte Occidentale d'Afrique (Sénégal au Cap de Monte, Archipels) par Valentim Fernandes (1506–10)*, pp. 25, 27.

N'Doye, M. C.
1947 " Le boeuf sacré de Diakaho (Sine-Saloum)." *Notes Africaines*, jan., No. 33, pp. 1–2.
1947 " Le culte de Tourou M'Bossé, Le Varan, divinité des pluies de semailles (Saloum, Sénégal)." *Notes Africaines*, jan., No. 33, pp. 2.
(Brief description of a ceremony designed to bring rain.)
1947 "Légende du Chasseur Sérère (Sine Saloum)." *Notes Africaines*, jan., No. 33, p. 23.
1947 " La mort d'un bour dans le Saloum." *Notes Africaines*, avr., No. 34 p. 27.
1948 " Le son du tabala dans le Rip." *Notes Africaines*, avr., No. 34 pp. 9–10.
(Describes drums with magical properties.)
1948 " La circoncision chez les Sérères-Sine." *Notes Africaines*., avr., No. 38 p. 21.

Pellissier, P.
1953 " Les paysans Sérères." *Les Cahiers d'Outre Mer.*, No. 22, pp. 105–27.
(An analysis of their ecology.)

R. G. V.
1814 *L'Afrique, ou histoire, moeurs, usages et coutumes des Africains*, pp. 93.

Sabatié, A.
n.d. *Le Sénégal, sa conquête et son organisation (1364–1925)*, pp. 190–1, 299.
1926 ?

Tautain, L.
1885 " Études critiques sur l'ethnologie et l'ethnographie des peuples du bassin du Sénégal." *Revue d'Ethnographie*, IV, p. 68.

Valtaud,
1922 " Coutume funéraire des Sérères." *Bull. du Com. d'Études Hist. et Scient.*, p. 251.

INDEX

Adultery, 60
Age groups, sets, 44, 53, 94
Agriculture, 29–34, 70, 94, 100
Aku, 79
Arabic, Arabs, 12, 24, 79

Bainunka, 98, 99
Bambara, 14, 35, 95, 98
Berbers, 12
Betrothal, 65–6
Birth, 62
British, 20, 21, 79
Burial, 45, 58, 68–9, 102

Calendar, farming, 33
Cattle, 31, 33–4, 58, 100
Character, 74–5, 93–4
Chiefs, chieftainship, 16–21 *passim*, 55–8, 101
Children, 60, 62–3, 64, 69, 74, 76, 77, 78, 98
Christianity, 26, 72, 98, 102
Circles, stone, 16
Circumcision, 55, 64–5, 101
Climate, 28
Coos, a Gambian term for millet, 40 (diagr.)
Crafts, 39–40
Creoles, 79
Crops, 29, 30–4 *passim*, 94, 101
Cults, 71, 72, 95, 103

Dances, dancing, 65, 75, 76, 95, 103
Death, 68–9, 102
Descent groups, 46–50, 94
Divination, 71
Divorce, 59–60
Dress, 73–4, 80, 103
Drink, 38–9, 70
Drumming, drums, 76–7

Education, 70, 71, 79
Etiquette, 75
Evil eye, 63, 75, 95

Fishing, 36, 93, 94, 101
Food, 37–8, 75
Friendship, 55
French, vii, 14, 17, 19, 20, 21, 79, 80, 93
Fulbe, 11, 12, 14, 15, 16, 17, 26, 33, 34, 35, 41, 42, 44, 58, 63, 64, 74, 76, 77, 79, 93, 95, 98, 99

Games, 77–8, 80
Gelowar, 14, 19, 20, 45, 46, 56
Gewel (griots), 25, 26, 40, 44, 45, 46, 57, 69, 74, 75, 80, 102

Headman, village, 45, 52
History, 16–21, 93, 99, 101
Homicide, 59
Homosexuality, 80
Horsemanship, 78

Houses, 41–3, 76, 94, 98
Hunting, 36
Hygiene, 75–6

Implements, 29–30 (diagr.)
Inheritance, 60–1, 94, 102
Islam, vii, 14, 20, 26, 38, 39, 45, 53, 59, 60, 61, 64-9 *passim*, 70, 71, 72, 94–5, 102

Joking relationships, 54–5, 99
Jola, vii, 14, 33, 34, 41, 53, 54, 77, 95, 98, 99, 100

Kinship terminology, 51
Kola nuts, 39, 66, 69

Labour, division of, 34–5
Land tenure, 35, 101
Language, 15, 22–7, 93, 97, 99–100
Lanterns, 78
Laube, 36, 44, 57
Law, 58–60
Lebanese, 79
Lebu, 22, 63, 79, 93–5
Literature, 24–7
Livestock, 33–4, 94

Mandinka, vii, 11, 12, 14, 15, 16, 19, 29, 34, 36, 41, 42, 53, 61, 63, 64, 71, 73, 75, 76, 77, 93, 98, 99, 101 (n.), 103 (n.)
Manjago, 15
Markets, 36
Marriage, 39, 45, 46, 52, 53–4 58, 59–60, 65–8, 80, 102
Matriliny, 19, 46–50 *passim*, 94, 101–2
Mauretanians, vii, 11, 14, 15, 16, 19, 20, 22, 36, 70, 79, 95
Migrations, 12–14, 52–3
Missions, see Christianity
Mourides, 14, 26, 41, 70, 95
Musical instruments, 77

Names, naming, 62–4
Nomenclature, tribal, 11, 97
Nyominka, 20, 98

Physical characteristics, 15, 93, 98
Play-acting, 77
Political systems, 55–8, 94, 101
Population figures, 12, 93, 95, 97, 98
Portugal, Portuguese, 17, 78, 79
Prostitution, 80

Rainfall, 12, 14, 28
Rain-making, 72, 103
Religion, 70–2, 94–5, 102–3

Salt-making, 94
Serahuli, 14, 25, 29, 35, 36, 42, 76, 98

INDEX

Serer, vii, 12, 14, 16, 20, 33, 54, 63, 69, 93, 95, 97–103
Settlements, 13 (diagr.), 14, 41, 98
Singing, 77
Slavery, slaves, 14, 36, 44, 45, 46, 59, 72, 98, 101 (n.)
Smiths, 39, 40, 44, 45, 52, 57, 69, 76
Social conditions, changing, 79–80, 95
Social organization, 44–55, 94, 101–2
Soils, 14
Spirit possession, spirits, 71–2, 95, 102–3
States, Wolof, 17, 18 (map), 19, 97, 101
Stratification, social, 44–6
Superstitions, 75, 76
Susu, 77, 95

Tattooing, 103
Theft, 59

Tobacco, 39
Totemism, 63, 73
Trade, 36, 53, 79, 101
Traditions, tribal, 14, 16–21, 93, 98–9
Transport, 80
Trial by ordeal, 59, 101
Tukulor (Torobe), vii, 14, 20, 70, 71, 98

Vegetation, 28
Villages, 14, 40 (diagr.), 51–2

Widows, 61, 69, 103
Witchcraft, 52, 59, 62, 63, 71, 95, 103
Women, 39, 73, 76, 77, 95; —status of, 58, 75, 80, 94, 101; —work of, 34–5, 36, 40, 94, 101
Wrestling, 77

SUPPLEMENTARY BIBLIOGRAPHIES

Since 1957, the major contributions to Wolof studies have been primarily in the linguistic field. Pichl (1961–3) has provided a series of Wolof texts (stories, songs, riddles, proverbs, etc.); Manessy and Sauvageot have collected and re-published a number of the older articles on Wolof and Serer (1963); Sauvageot has produced an excellent study of the language (1965), while recently an Introductory Course in Dakar Wolof has been made available by the Center for Applied Linguistics in Washington (1966).

A useful summary of Senegalese history has been compiled by Brigaud (1962), and a detailed account of the history of Kayor provided by Monteil (1963).

A good article on the Wolof of Bas-Ferlo has been written by Audiger (1961), while David Ames has continued to produce articles based on his field work in the Gambia in the early nineteen-fifties.

DAVID P. GAMBLE
August 1966

WOLOF
BIBLIOGRAPHY OF LINGUISTIC MATERIAL
VOCABULARIES, DICTIONARIES, GRAMMARS, ETC.

1828 Kilham, Hannah
Specimens of African languages spoken in the Colony of Sierra Leone. Committee of the Society of Friends for Promoting African Instruction. (This contains the numerals and some 70 words in Wolof. The lists for each language were published on separate sheets about 1830.)

1848 Clarke, J.
Specimens of dialects. Short vocabularies of languages and notes of countries and customs in Africa. (Examples of Wolof from Mollien and Kilham, as well as those collected by Clarke.)

1854 Koelle, S. W.
Polyglotta Africana, etc. (Contains a list of Wolof words.)

1877 Cust, R. N.
A sketch of the modern languages of Africa. (Vol. I, pp. 173–5.)

1883 Hovelacque, A.
The science of language, linguistics, philosophy, etymology. Translated by A. H. **Leane.** (Wolof: pp. 52–6.)

1903 Rambaud, J-B.
" Les pronoms personnels et les possessifs en Wolof." *Bull. de la Soc. de Linguistique de Paris,* T.12, cxvi–cxx.

1911–13 Migeod, F. W. H.
The languages of West Africa. 2 vols. (Specimens of Wolof, pp. 242–3.)

1929 Coustenoble, Mlle H.
" Quelques observations sur la prononciation de la langue Wolof (Sénégal)". *Le Maître phonétique,* jan-fév., 1929, pp. 1–2. (Reprinted in Manessy et Sauvageot: *Wolof et Sérèr* (1963).)

1933 Butavand, F.
" Études de linguistique africaine et asiatique comparée." (Wolof, pp. 26–34.)

1947 Cadenat, Jean
"Noms vernaculaires des principales formes d'animaux marins des Côtes d'Afrique occidentale Française." *I.F.A.N. Catalogues II.*

1947 Mouradian, J.
" Note de sémantique négro-africaine." *Notes Africaines,* No. 34, pp. 13–14.

1948 Homburger, L.
" De l'origine des classes nominales dans les langues négro-africaines." *Lingua,* Vol. 1, 2, mars, pp. 235–246.

1956 Faye, J. C., and Sillah, M. A.
The orthography of Gambian Languages—Wolof and Mandinka. (Govt. Printer, Bathurst.)

1958 Gamble, D. P.
Wolof English-Dictionary. (Cyclostyled 19 p. Research Dept. Colonial Office. Remaining copies with Ministry of Local Government, Bathurst.)

1959 Gamble, D. P.
Elementary Wolof Grammar. (Cyclostyled 21 p. Research Dept. Colonial Office. Remaining copies with Ministry of Local Government, Bathurst.) Printed in Manessy & Sauvageot: *Wolof et Sérèr* (1963).

1959 Gamble, D. P.
" Chain-rhymes in Senegambian Languages." *Africa,* XXIX, Jan. 1959, pp. 82–3.

1963 Manessy, G., and Sauvageot, S.
Wolof et Sérèr. Etudes de phonétique et de grammaire descriptive. (Université de **Dakar.**) (An extremely useful collection of articles by Rambaud, Delafosse, Coustenoble, Labouret, Ward, Mouradian, Senghor, Ndiaye, Gamble, etc., reprinted from various journals.)

2   THE WOLOF OF SENEGAMBIA

1961–1963   Pichl, W.

In Afrika und Übersee

Wolof-Erzählungen	Bd. XLIV Heft 4	pp. 253–82
	Bd. XLV Heft 1–2	67–95
	Bd. XLV Heft 3	189–205
Ein Wolof-Gedicht und Lieder	Bd. XLV Heft 4	271–85
Wolof-Sprichwörter und Rätsel	Bd. XLVI Heft 1–2	93–109
Verschiedene Wolof-Texte	Bd. XLVI Heft 3	204–18

(A valuable collection of Wolof stories, songs, proverbs and riddles. Wolof text with German translation.)

1963   Sauvageot, S.
" Les classes nominales et leurs fonctions dans le groupe Sénégalo-Guinéen ou Ouest-Atlantique. 3. Wolof (Dialecte du Dyolof). Pp. 274–6 in *Actes du Second Colloque International de Linguistique Négro-Africaine. Dakar. 1962.*

1965   Sauvageot, S.
Description synchronique d'un dialecte wolof: Le parler du Dyolof.
(Mémoires de l'Institut Français d'Afrique Noire, No. 73, Dakar.) (An excellent study of the language.)

1966   Stewart, W. A., Babou, Cheikh, Pedtke, D., and others.
Introductory course in Dakar Wolof. Center for Applied Linguistics, Washington D.C.
(A massive tome of about 460 pages.)

RELIGIOUS LITERATURE

1824   *Second Report of the Committee Managing a Fund raised for the purpose of promoting African Instruction with an Appendix.* London (Society of Friends). (Contains a selection from the Holy Scriptures in Wolof and English, pp. 34–9.)

1862   *Linjil i Yisu Krista suñu borom bi.* Gospel of St. Matthew in Jolof. British and Foreign Bible Society.

1957   Fathers of the Congregation of the Holy Ghost, Bathurst. *The Catholic Hymn Book.*
(Contains Wolof hymns, pp. 137, 142, 147, 148.)

1957   Catholic Mission, Bathurst (Gambia).
Katesism (Volof.)

1964   *Yalla Wax Na* (16 pages). Société pour la distribution des Saintes Écritures, London.

Ames, D. W.
> **1953**   " Plural marriage among the Wolof in the Gambia: with a consideration of problems of marital adjustment and patterned ways of resolving tensions." Ph.D. thesis. Northwestern University.
>
> **1958**   " The dual function of the ' Little People ' of the forest in the lives of the Wolof." *Journal of American Folklore*, Jan.-Mar., Vol. 71, pp. 23–6.
>
> **1959**   " Wolof co-operative work groups." Ch. 12, pp. 224–37, in *Continuity and Change in African Cultures*, edited by W. R. Bascom and M. J. Herskovits.
>
> **1959**   " Belief in ' witches ' among the rural Wolof of the Gambia." *Africa*, XXIX, Jul., pp. 263–73.
>
> **1962**   " The rural Wolof of the Gambia." In *Markets in Africa*, edited by P. Bohannan and G. Dalton.

Ancelle, J.
> **1886**   *Les explorations au Sénégal et dans les contrées voisines*, etc.
> (Wolof, Ch. XXXII.)

Audiger, J.
> **1961**   " Les Ouolofs du Bas-Ferlo." *Les Cahiers d'Outre-Mer*, No. 54, pp. 157–81.
> (A useful article.)

Ba, T. O.
> **1957**   " Essai historique sur le Rip (Sénégal)." *Bull. de l'I.F.A.N.*, juil.-oct., XIX (B), pp. 564–91.

Basset, R.
> **1888–9**   " Folk Lore Wolof." *Melusine*, T.IV, pp. 58–9, 91–4, 132–3, 234–5.

Bérenger-Féraud, L.S-B.
> 'Etude sur les griots des peuplades de la Sénégambie', *Revue d'Anthropologie*, pp. 266–79.
>
> **1883**   " Le marriage chez les Nègres Sénégambiens."
> *Revue d'Anthropologie*, pp. 284–98.

Brigaud, F.
> **1962**   *Histoire traditionnelle du Sénégal.*
> (Etudes Sénégalaises, No. 9. Saint-Louis.)

Carrere, F. and Holle, P.
> *De la Sénégambie française.*

BIBLIOGRAPHIES

Cisse, D.
1947 " La mort du Damel." *Présence Africaine, nov.-déc.*, pp. 62–77.
(A play in French based on tradition.)

Cottrell, K.
1958 *More than Sunburnt.* (Contains drawings of Wolof of Dakar.)

Crowder, M.
1959 *Pagans and Politicians.*
1959 " Gamou at Tivouane." *West African Review*, Oct., pp. 634–5.
(Description of the annual Muslim festival of the Tidjane sect.)

D'Anfreville de la Salle
1912 *Sur la Côte d'Afrique.*

Deniker, J. & Laloy, L.
1889 *Les races exotiques à l'exposition Universelle de* 1889. (Wolof, pp. 263–5.)

de Rochebrune, A. T.
1881 " La femme et l'enfant dans la race ouolove." *Revue d'anthropologie*, pp. 260–94.
(Mainly physical anthropology.)

Diop, Cheikh A.
1955 *Nations nègres et culture.*

Diop, B.
1947 *Les contes d'Amadou Koumba.*
1949 " Le pretexte " (Wolof story). *Présence Africaine.* 6, pp. 94–99
1949 " La cuiller sale " (Wolof story). *Présence Africaine*, 6, pp. 100–107.
1951 " Un cousinage ". (Wolof story). *Présence Africaine*, 12, pp. 189–201.
1958 *Les nouveaux contes d'Amadou Koumba.*

Dupré, Capt. E. P. F.
1933 " La campagne du Cayor en 1883." *Rev. d'hist. des colonies*, pp. 251–92. (Letters
edited by Rene Servatius. Introduction by A. Martineau.)

Falade, S.
1960 " Femmes de Dakar et de son agglomération." In *Femmes d'Afrique Noire*, edited
by Denise Paulme.
(English translation published 1963.)

Fouquet, J.
1958 " La traite des arachides dans le pays de Kaolack, et ses conséquences économiques,
sociales et juridiques." (*Etudes Sénégalasies*, No. 8, Saint-Louis.)

Friends, Society of,
1822 Report of the Committee Managing a Fund raised by some friends for the puprose
of promoting African Instruction; with an account of a visit to the Gambia and
Sierra Leone.

Griaule, M.
1938 " Histoires wolof." *Cahiers de Sud*, 268, pp. 629–6.

Hautefeuille, L. B.
1830 *Plan de colonisation des possessions françaises dans l'Afrique occidentale.*

Hewett, J. F. N.
1862 *European settlements on the West Coast of Africa*, etc.

Jaeger, P.
1943 " Le Heeria insignis. Ce qu'en pensent les indigènes du Saloum." *Notes Africaines*,
juillet, p. 8.

Jobe, B. O.
n.d. (?1964) " Child-naming ceremony among the Wollofs." *S.P.A.C.* (Magazine of the
Society for the Promotion of African Culture). Fourah Bay College, Sierra
Leone. Vol. II, No. 1, pp. 12–13.

Labouret, H.
1929 " La parenté à plaisanteries en Afrique occidentale." *Africa*, II, July, pp. 244–53.

Lawrie, Jean
1960 *The marriage of Gor. The true account of a white girl's life with a black man.* (The
life of a Wolof from Bathurst, living in a condemned hovel in the East End of
London.)

Lèques, R.
1957 " La mode actuelle chez les Dakaroises (Étude de psychologie sociale)" *Bull. de
l'I.F.A.N.*, XIX, juil-oct., pp. 431–42.

Leye, T.
1957 " Interpretation de quelques noms d'insectes en langue Wolof." *Notes Africaines*, avr.,
pp. 42–3.

McCallum, J. K.
1907 *Laws and customs of the Jolluf people.* (McCarthy Island Province.) (Typescript.
23 pp. Copy at Royal Anthropological Institute, London.)

Marty, P.
1924 " L'expédition de Repentigny dans le Saloum et la première cession du pays à la
France en 1785." *Revue de l'histoire des Colonies Françaises*, pp. 43–66.

THE WOLOF OF SENEGAMBIA

Masse, L.
1957 " Contribution à l'étude de la ville de Thiès II." *Bull. de l'I.F.A.N.*, XIX (B), pp. 275–83.

Maugham, R. F. C.
1939 " Some native races of West Africa. The Wolofs of Senegal." *West African Review*, March, pp. 15–16.

Mauny, R.
1956 *Esmeraldo de Situ Orbis (Côte Occidentale d'Afrique du Sud Marocain au Gabon) par Duarte Pacheco Pereira (vers 1506–1508).* Centro de Estudos de Guiné Portuguesa, No. 19. Bissau.

Monteil, V.
1963 " Lat Dior, Damel de Kayor (1842–1886) et l'islamisation des Wolofs." *Archives de Sociologie des Religions*, 16, juil.-dec., pp. 77–104.

N'Diaye, M.
1961 " Les débuts du règne." *La Vie Africaine*, No. 11, pp. 20–3, No. 12, pp. 21–3, No. 13, pp. 21–4.
(A play dealing with Baol towards the end of the xviith century.)

Pichard
1865 " La Gambie." *Revue Maritime et Coloniale*, XIV, pp. 225–60.

Price, J. H.
1959 " Some notes on the influence of women in Gambian politics." In *Conference Proceedings: Nigerian Institute of Social and Economic Research*, Dec. 1958.

Rancon, A.
1894 *Dans la Haute Gambie. Voyage d'exploration scientifique*, 1891–92.

Renzi, A.
1842 " Les Ouolofs." *L'Investigateur, Journal de l'Institut historique*, pp. 401–4.

Robin, J.
1944 " Une corvée villageoise à Dagana." *Notes Africaines*, No. 23, juin, pp. 7–8.
1945 " Le Marbat: marché au bétail de Louga." *Africa*, XV, pp. 47–59.

Sadji, A.
1958 *Maimouna.* (A novel about a village girl who goes to Dakar. Describes the period before the Second World War.)

Savonnet, G.
1952 " Evolution démographique de la ville de Thiès." *Notes Africaines*, No. 56, pp. 122–4.

Schefer, C.
1895 *Relation des voyages à la Côte occidentale d'Afrique d'Alvise de Ca'da Mosto.* 1455–57. (Contains interesting material on the Wolof.)

Silla, Ousmane
1964 " Le système des castes dans la société oulof." *France-Eurafrique*, Vol. 16, No. 148, janv., pp. 38–40.

Sow, A.
1962 " Monographie du village de Cambérène (Sénégal)." *Notes Africaines*, avr., pp. 51–60.

Thiam, B.
1950 " La coiffure ' Gossi ' et les bijoux qui lui sont assortis. *Notes Africaines*, No. 45, pp. 9–11.
1952 " Le Dieungue ou anneau de cheville d'esclave." *Notes Africaines*, No. 53, p. 13.

Thore, L.
1964 " Mariage et divorce dans la banlieu de Dakar." *Cahiers d'Etudes Africaines*, Vol. IV, pp. 479–551.

Verneau
" Ouolofs, Leybous et Sérères." *L'Anthropologie*, VI, pp. 510–28. (Physical anthropology.)

LEBU BIBLIOGRAPHY

Adande, A.
1951 " Origine des villages de Yombeul et Tiaroye (Sénégal)." *Notes Africaines*, avr., pp. 56.

Anon.
1951 "Vers une évolution du mariage sénégalais." *Bull. I.F.A.N.*, T.13, pp. 542–6.

Balandier, G.
1966 *Ambiguous Africa.* (See Chapters II and III.)

Monod, A.
1950 " Sur un jouet Lebou: Le " Crabe." *Notes Africaines*, avr. p. 44.

Monod, Th.
1947 " Sur un détail du gréement de la pirogue Wolof-Lébu (Sénégal)." 2 *Conferencia International dos Africanistas ocidentais.* Bissau, pp. 105–116.

Sy. Eliane
1965 " Cayar, village de pêcheurs-cultivateurs au Sénégal." *Les Cahiers d'Outre-Mer*, oct.-déc., pp. 342–68. (Wolof–Lebu.)

BIBLIOGRAPHIES

SERER LINGUISTIC BIBLIOGRAPHY

Butavand, F.
1933   *Études de linguistique africaine et asiatique comparée.* (Serer, pp. 35–42.)

Destaing, E.
1910–11 " Note de phonétique (Afrique occidentale)". *Memoires de la Société de Linguistique de Paris,* pp. 289–99.

Hestermann, F.
1912   " Der Anlautwechsel in der Serersprache in Senegambien, Westafrika." *Wiener Zeitschrift für die Kunde des Morgenlandes,* XXVI, pp. 350–62. (Reprinted in Manessy and Sauvageot: *Wolof et Sérèr.*)

Manessy, G., and Sauvageot, S.
1963   *Wolof et Sérèr. Études de phonétique et de grammaire descriptive.* Université de Dakar. (Reprints articles by Faidherbe, Hestermann, Senghor, and Ezanno.)

Pichl, W.
1963   " La permutation et l'accord en Sérèr." In *Actes du Second Colloque International de Linguistique Négro-africaine, Dakar.* 1962. pp. 78–85.
" Les classes nominales et leurs fonctions dans le groupe Sénégalo-guinéen ou ouest-Atlantique." *Ibid.,* pp. 271–3.

For religious works consult the bibliography in Manessy and Sauvageot (1963).

SERER GENERAL BIBLIOGRAPHY

Duchemin, G-J.
1945   " Exemples de substitution de mythes avec maintien du rite dans les croyances animistes au Sénégal et au Fouta-Djallon." In *Ire Conférence Internationale des Africanistes de l'Ouest. Dakar,* T.II, pp. 351–3.

1947   " L'organisation religieuse et son rôle politique dans le royaume sérère du Sine (Sénègal). In 2. *Conferencia International dos Africanistas ócidentais,* pp. 367–76.

N'Diaye, S.
1964   " Notes sur les engins de pêche chez les Sérèr." *Notes Africaines,* oct. pp. 116–120.

O'Connor, Col. L. S.
1859   " Account of a visit to the King of Bur Sin, 64 miles to the North of the Gambia." *Proc. Roy. Geog. Soc.,* III, pp. 377–9.

Pinet-Laprade
1865   " Notice sur les Sérères." *Revue Maritime et Coloniale,* T.XIII, pp. 479–92, 709–2.8.